IN A
WILD
PLACE

A Natural History
of High Ledges

IN A
WILD
PLACE

A Natural History
of High Ledges

·

Ellsworth Barnard

Ellsworth Barnard

with wood engravings by

Charles H. Joslin

Charles H. Joslin

Massachusetts Audubon Society

**Library of Congress
Cataloging-in-Publication Data**

Barnard, Ellsworth, 1907—
    In a wild place / by Ellsworth Barnard; with illustrations
by Charles H. Joslin.
    p.   cm.
  Includes index.
  ISBN 0-932691-22-6
  1. Natural history—Massachusetts—High Ledges Wildlife
Sanctuary.
  2. High Ledges Wildlife Sanctuary (Mass.)
  I. Title.
QH105.M4B37 1998
508.744´22—dc21   97-516
                                                                            CIP
Massachusetts Audubon Society   Lincoln, Massachusetts

To the memory of

Nancy McMaster

who loved High Ledges

Contents

Foreword by John Hanson Mitchell

WOODBLOCKS

Cover Art: White Oak

Foreword

by John Hanson Mitchell

Years ago I heard a story about a man in our town who was the sort of resident naturalist that every rural or suburban community seems to produce. Some neighbor had been telling grand stories of his travels across America to a group of people at a party and asked the naturalist if he had done any traveling over the summer. He had, he said. "I made it halfway across my backyard."

This kind of singular devotion to a small area, the exploration of the wildness of the nearby, is the stuff that all great naturalists share. Gilbert White devoted volume after volume of his letters to the countryside around Selborne in Hampshire, England, an area that he rarely left. The famous French entomologist Jean-Henri Fabre carried out many of his studies around Carpentras and Avignon in the south of France. Eliot Howard's discovery of the phenomenon of territory in birds was revealed by the close studies of the birds around his estate, Clareland, in the English Midlands. Thoreau, as he himself facetiously noted, traveled much—in Concord! John Burroughs devoted himself to the Hudson River valley, John Muir to the Sierras, Aldo Leopold to Sand County. With a few exceptions (John James Audubon and Charles Darwin being prime candidates), great naturalists never go anywhere. They don't have to; the world is in their own backyard.

The tradition of sounding the deeper meanings of local environments is much more ancient than the recent phenomenon of Western culture; however, Chinese poets of the eighth century had a passion

for pure nature that has not yet been matched for its intensity. Their ideal was to return to the fastness of mountain retreats, there to live with the natural procession of the seasons. The Chinese character *shan shui,* which literally means mountains and rivers, implies the whole range of this experience, something akin to landscape of all of nature. The Spanish have a word with a similar connotation, *querencia,* which implies a sense of place or familiarity with the nature of a place. The Hopi have a comparable phrase, *tuwanasaapi,* which means center of the universe, the special place, the place where you belong.

Allegiance to place is best realized by those who have grown up in an area and have remained there over the course of a lifetime—those who, in the words of the Chinese poets, have come to know the seasons of a place, the flowering of the wild plants, the snows and rains of winter and spring. But rarely in this mobile American age, in which the frontier and the fast lane hold sway, does one run across a work that celebrates the local at a deep level. *In a Wild Place* is such a work. It is a celebration of the natural history of a small, obscure piece of the planet in western Massachusetts.

Ellsworth Barnard, better known to his friends and allies as Dutch, has had a long and active life, much of it concentrated on one small tract of land of some six-hundred-acres, known locally as High Ledges, set above the Deerfield River in the town of Shelburne, Massachusetts. Barnard grew up in Shelburne, on a farm adjacent to land that is now High Ledges Wildlife Sanctuary. From an early age, thanks in part to a nature-loving mother, he took to exploring the nature of the lands around his family farm and developed a bond with the land, which, as is often the case in such situations, was never broken. In the 1920s Barnard left the farm for academia and for years was a dedicated professor of English, sharing with his students at the University of Massachusetts and other colleges and universities his love of great literature and his respect for clear and honest writing. Along the way, he published critical studies of Shelley and the American poet Edwin Arlington Robinson, as well as an authoritative biography of Wendell Willkie.

But, though he taught in places as remote from one another as Florida, Michigan, and Maine, he and his wife, Mary, always returned to what they regarded as their real home, High Ledges. Then in 1940 he and his wife bought a 60-acre tract of land adjoining the family farm where he grew up, which included the geological feature known locally as High Ledges. Over the next few decades they added to the original lot, ending in 1967 with the purchase of 150 acres of the old Barnard family farm. In 1970, they donated the total of 400 acres to the Massachusetts Audubon Society. The Sanctuary holdings have now been expanded to nearly six-hundred-acres, and the Barnards continue to live on the plot in summer in a house on the cliffs, with a view west across the valley of the Deerfield.

To those who know the place, High Ledges is a very special area; many who go there are enchanted after the first walk and return in all seasons. One of these visitors was the wood-engraving artist Charles Joslin who lives in the nearby town of Charlemont. In the late 1980s, Joslin asked Dutch Barnard if he would be interested in writing a book about the tract, which would be illustrated by his wood engravings. The result of this collaboration is the book that follows.

Although the essays, like the illustrations, take their inspiration from High Ledges, they should appeal to all lovers of nature. The Sanctuary is indeed unique, but the varied habitat creates a concentration of plant species rarely found in a single area of similar size; for instance, there are some twenty species of native orchids on the 700-acre tract. Moreover, the accounts of the particular species of plants and animals that High Ledges offers have an appeal apart from their local associations.

But there is more to High Ledges than the plants and animals of the various habitats. It is worth noting perhaps that both these men were well along in years when this project was undertaken. The fact that they would proceed with an endeavor that requires a great deal of tramping around wetlands and steep slopes in all seasons to observe the wildlife and the plants, and then exert the energy to produce the text and prints, says something about the enduring draw—the force, really—that is engendered in High Ledges. The Hopi would say they had found *tuwanasaapi*.

IN A
WILD
PLACE

A Natural History
of High Ledges

CHAPTER 1

The View from the Ledges

There is a spot along the crest of the ridge that, in the town of Shelburne, forms the steep eastern slope of the Deerfield River valley, where a rock fall in some distant past has left an overhanging cliff known locally as the High Ledges. Traditionally, this was a favorite destination for hikers from the nearby town of Shelburne Falls; and I remember hearing from my father that there was once a road leading to it from the Barnard farm along which one could drive a horse and buggy.

Visitors to the site were more than rewarded for the effort. Indeed, though "breathtaking" is a trite term, many first-time visitors have found it accurate. Facing a little south of west, one looks down almost a thousand feet to the village with its toylike houses peeping out from among the sugar maples that in summer shade the streets and in autumn flame with color. Beyond, the hills of Buckland rise sharply to the still higher summits of the town of Ashfield. I remember that long ago there was one bare, rounded crest along which a line of trees, standing out against the sky, suggested the march of a camel caravan across the desert. But half a century of new growth has erased the image.

A mile or two north of the village, the river makes an abrupt turn to the west; and from High Ledges one can look straight up its *v*-shaped valley, with a series of ridges running down to the river on either side, each one rising beyond the other toward the level line topping the Hoosac range—a line broken, beyond, by the massive upward surge of Mount Greylock toward a perfect dome whose summit is the highest point in Massachusetts.

This is the panorama when the air is clear and the face of nature is unshadowed. But the scene is ever-changing from season to season, from day to day, from hour to hour. In winter the leafless trees on near hillsides stand stark against the snow, except for dark green stands of pines and hemlocks. Spring clothes the landscape with a luminous mist of pale green, which yields to summer's full-blown leafy garment of deeper hue. And this in turn, as the days grow shorter and the nights take on a chill, gives way to a reckless riot of color as the earth celebrates the completion of another cycle of life and growth.

No less dramatic than the changes of the seasons are those decreed by the weather. On warm summer days, Greylock disappears in the haze, and sometimes the features of even the nearer hills and ridges melt into a soft blur; or when a northeast storm settles in, one can look out into a blank gray impenetrable mist that gives no hint of what may lie beyond, as if the top of the cliff were the edge of the world. Or, foreshadowing fair weather, the morning mist may fill the valley like a sea of white beneath a clear blue sky; and then in a moment it lifts and vanishes like a dream, and the valley wakes to reality under the climbing sun.

Or on some sultry summer afternoon, a cloud may appear on the western horizon and quickly rise and spread, darkening as it grows, and presently open below to a gray rain curtain that marches down the river, blotting out ridge after ridge as it comes—until the whole valley is hidden and torrents of rain begin to lash the western windows of the house, which stands a few yards back from the edge of the cliff. Once, however, I remember that the cloud did not open as it advanced, so that it hung like a huge dark shroud above the cliff; and just at that moment a flock of migrating nighthawks crossed in front of it, the white patches on their wings startlingly distinct against the seemingly solid wall of black.

On other occasions, the gathering of a storm is signaled by lightning flashes along the horizon accompanied by the low rumble of thunder, growing brighter and louder as the storm approaches, until finally, blinding and deafening, it hurls itself in unobstructed fury against the mountain wall. On more than one of the ancient red pines anchored in cracks in the rock wall, there is visible a long scar running down the trunk where a bolt of lightning found a convenient path to the earth.

Presently, however, the storm passes, and, while the thunder still mutters to the east, the clouds open beyond Greylock; and the descending sun casts its tranquil rays across the hills and through the valley, creating infinitely varied light effects (once, I remember, a gathering of thin, luminous, crimson mist).

And of course the wide horizon offers a matchless view—framed, if one moves back a little from the edge of the cliff, by dark pines—of the sunset, whether radiant beneath a cloudless sky, or canopied by curtains of rose or gold or other tones and tints that only nature can create.

And under a full moon the landscape is transformed into a fairyland, inviting one to venture beyond the confines of earth-bound existence.

Though the view from the High Ledges proper is the most spectacular feature of this six-hundred-acre tract called High Ledges Wildlife Sanctuary and the magnet that draws a majority of the visitors, there are other features that contribute scarcely less to making the area truly unique. The ridge on whose crest the special lookout point is located is only one of several roughly parallel rock formations running north and south, perhaps carved by the glacier, with steep west-

ern faces, and terraces between, that dominate the topography of the northern and western parts of the Sanctuary, so that in some places the land descends as if by giant steps to the valley floor.

The substratum that in this area underlies the thin soil and bares itself on the faces of the cliffs is mostly an ancient schist, a metamorphic crystalline rock sometimes containing tiny garnets and flakes of mica, and occasionally interveined with quartz or other minerals. From this, the forces of nature have produced in various places unexpected formations, of which the most remarkable is the Wolves' Den. Here, the face of a low cliff is deeply penetrated by several tunnels with roughly rectangular openings, angling slightly downward and diminishing in size, ending, to the eye of the viewer, in a mass of dead leaves and other debris. How these were formed is a question that nobody has been able to

answer. According to local legend, which there seems no reason to question, here was the lair of the area's last family of wolves, until they were hunted down and destroyed by farmers angered by their depredations.

Among other striking geological features is Table Rock, one of a number of large boulders deposited in various places by the glacier. Distinguished by its nearly cubical shape, each smooth face forms an approximate square some three feet on a side. Resting on a flat ledge at the top of an elevated piece of land, it was once, when the area was an open pasture, a convenient landmark, but now it is lost in the woods that have asserted their ancient claim to the land.

In contrast to the rugged topography of the western part of the Sanctuary, the eastern part is a rolling plateau, where the bedrock, though never far below the surface, emerges only occasionally. Once mainly pasture land with open fields and grassy slopes, it is now returning to the original unbroken forest, except for limited areas kept open artificially to provide the special habitat required by certain species of plants and animals that would otherwise be lost. Adding to the variety of this part of the Sanctuary is an alder swamp of about two acres—designated the Orchid Swamp because four species of orchids grow there, besides the pink lady's slippers along the edge. Here, also, as elsewhere around the Sanctuary, are smaller wetlands scattered about, each with its own distinctive character.

This extraordinary diversity of terrain and habitat gives rise to a corresponding diversity of plant and animal species, some representative of the general area, some relatively rare. The woods that cover most of the Sanctuary contain all the common northern hardwoods: sugar and red maple; red, white, and black oak; black, white, yellow, and gray birch; shagbark hickory and pignut, a relative with smooth bark and bitter nuts; two species of aspen (quaking and bigtooth, with reference to the leaves); white and black ash; four trees unrelated except that their popular names begin with *b*, beech, basswood, butternut, and black cherry; ironwood, or hop hornbeam; an occasional young elm, safe so far from Dutch elm disease; and the American chestnut, which is gradually triumphing over the chestnut blight.

Here and there among the deciduous trees are stands of evergreens—chiefly white pine and hemlock, though, in the area of the High Ledges proper, it is the red pine that is dominant, a species rare in Massachusetts. Three other species of evergreens—red cedar, red spruce, and balsam fir—are also found on the Sanctuary, but only as scattered individuals.

It is to be regretted that no trees on the Sanctuary are fully mature, except for a few relatively small and short-lived species, or an occasional giant oak or maple whose wide-spreading branches—a sign of its having grown to maturity on open land—have made it valueless for lumber. Even the areas that were never cleared have been repeatedly cutover since colonial times (once by my father at the beginning of this century). Even so, some have reached a size to stir the heart of a lover of trees.

Still, from a human point of view, one would not wish the entire Sanctuary to return to its primeval state. Many shrubs and small woody plants that charm the visitor's eye, and provide a specific habitat for many forms of animal life, flourish only in full sunlight or along the forest border. Steeplebush and meadowsweet, for instance, with their respective blooms of pink and white, would vanish; as would sweet fern (not a fern but a flowering plant related to the bayberry), whose leaves when crushed give off a wonderful aromatic fragrance; swamp pink, a native azalea with plumes of pink blossoms that exhale an intoxicating, spicy sweetness; and mountain laurel, whose glossy leaves frame seemingly solid masses of pink and white. The last of these will also grow in open woods, but rarely flower in shade—although on rare occasions they burst into bloom and fill the forest with a sea of white.

Other shrubs or small trees, however, happily accommodate themselves to their natural surroundings where the woods are thinned by dry and rocky, or wet and heavy, soil. In favored spots around the Sanctuary, especially near the Ledges proper, the uniform tint of the awakening April woods is dramatically punctuated by the white blossoms of various species of shadbush, often called juneberry or serviceberry. The taller ones stand out like clear white candle flames, the flowers followed by berries that provide a banquet for many birds—cedar waxwings, hermit thrushes, rose-breasted grosbeaks, and scarlet tanagers, among others.

And in autumn, when the surrounding foliage has assumed its seasonal tones of red and gold, the twigs on clumps of witch hazel give

birth to tiny flowers with slender, pale yellow petals portending small spherical capsules that, the following summer, will explode and spray the minute seeds over the surrounding area.

But, despite the strong appeal to sense and spirit of the Sanctuary's trees and shrubs, the property's unique distinction lies in its wealth of species of nonwoody flowering plants—those whose winter death and springtime resurrection have through the centuries strengthened the human challenge to the finality of death.

This is a subject for a book of its own. Here I can only hint at the prodigality of nature's offerings as the seasons change. First, in early April, come mayflowers (trailing arbutus) with their elusive and enchanting fragrance, and hepaticas, whose white or pastel-colored blossoms brighten the brown forest floor. Then, early yellow violets (celebrated by William Cullen Bryant in a little poem that charmed me as a child), the first to blossom of the nine violet species native to the Sanctuary. Next, in late April and early May, come trilliums, red and painted, and the improbable flowers of the jack-in-the-pulpit; in late May and early June, the still more fantastic shapeliness of pink and yellow lady's slippers; and in mid-June, pitcher plants with their exotic blood-red blossoms, and leaves whose still more strange design, offering fatal temptation to passing insects, make it hard to deny intelligence to the evolutionary process of which it is the result.

July is ushered in by tall-stemmed lilies with whorls of glossy leaves, and flowers, one or several, whose splendor instantly attracts the eye: those of the Canada lily gracefully nodding, bell shaped, yellow with dusky dots; those of the wood lily a flaring orange-red with bold black spots that stand with military erectness.

Midsummer's flowers seem generally more subdued. Even the most visible of the orchids, the purple fringed and ragged fringed, charm more by their delicacy than their ornate elegance. A similar diffidence appears in the gentians, fringed and closed, that welcome the morning sun as fall approaches. But by autumn this trait is absent in the riot of asters and goldenrod—some dozen species of each—which bring a dramatic close to nature's annual parade of flowers.

This rich variety extends to the nonflowering plants: four species of clubmosses that cover the ground with an evergreen carpet; thirty species of ferns, from the tiny maidenhair spleenwort that shyly emerges from cracks in sheer rock faces to the great head-high clusters of cinnamon ferns that turn the Orchid Swamp into a jungle where the explorer may get lost; and mushrooms and fungi that appear on the woodland floor, varying in size from one with a cap not much larger than a pinhead to one the size of a luncheon plate, ranging through all the colors of the rainbow except green, as well as pure white and numerous shades of gray and brown, and offering, in some species, a delight to the gourmet, but in others, death to the careless consumer.

As for animate life, there are the butterflies that no eye can miss and reptiles—turtles and snakes—more seldom seen, though a garter snake makes its home under the front doorstep of the house. I have fished a ringneck snake out of the rain barrel, and a shed skin, shining and transparent, has mysteriously appeared beside the fireplace. Then there are the amphibians—frogs, toads, and salamanders. I listen each spring for the opening chorus of wood frogs and the music of spring

peepers, and children are always delighted by finding, along the trails after a rain, red-spotted newts.

Children are most excited, however, by seldom-seen mammals—like the porcupine that once enthralled a group of second graders at the beginning of a nature walk. And always fascinating, to all ages, are the beavers whose massive dam has created a small lake at the foot of the mountain along the western edge of the Sanctuary, visited on occasion by minks and otters. As for other mammalian dwellers on the Sanctuary, deer are, of course, a universal favorite of animal lovers, though lovers of flowers are less than charmed by their appetite for yellow lady's slippers and purple fringed orchids. On the other hand, few people are ever aware of the presence of many smaller mammals, such as tiny shorttail shrews, and are almost equally unlikely, at the other extreme in size, to encounter (as did one hiker on a Sanctuary trail) a bear. Large or small, however, and seen or unseen, mammals are ever-present participants, like other forms of life, in nature's endless drama—a drama for which it would be hard to imagine a better stage than the Sanctuary offers.

In this drama, to me, the most appealing participants have always been the birds. In them I find embodied the very essence of life—the harmony of color, the miracle of song, the grace of movement, the throbbing energy, the freedom and fragility of earthly existence.

The bluebirds, whose first, faint, skyborne calls announcing spring's return brought to me as a child the most magical moment of the year, now raise their broods in nesting boxes along the road. From the top of a nearby tree, a towhee may bid the visitor, *Drink your tea,* while a chestnut-sided warbler whose nest is in the low shrubbery at the woods' edge exclaims, *Pleased, pleased, pleased to meet yuh!* Seated at the edge of the cliff, one may hope to see hawks, vultures, and ravens soaring above the valley in the morning sun, as if to deride the earthbound existence of human beings. In the woods, a wanderer away from the beaten trails may suddenly be halted by a thunderous roar of wings as a grouse takes flight, or by a fluttering at his feet as an ovenbird deserts her neatly roofed nest. Or one may hear, accompanied by the gurgle of a brook through a deep ravine, the high, clear song of a winter wren rippling on and on like the stream itself. And at the Ledges, in the evening, one can hear from the pines along the cliff a hermit thrush in a song of unearthly sweetness, pronouncing a benediction on the departing day.

So, here is one small, precious piece of earth that will remain unspoiled, where refugees from the restless rush of the human world may find in the presence of nature a moment of peace.

CHAPTER 2

Nature's Altered Face

The unique appeal of High Ledges varies with the seasons but is never absent. Though many visitors find most poignant the bursting buds and rapturous songs of spring, and others are most deeply stirred by the flaming colors and the sense of fulfillment that autumn offers, winter also has its charm. In the distance, the dome of Greylock gleams white against the blue of the sky, while near at hand the sharply outlined tree trunks frame unsuspected vistas and the rocky faces of ledges are unveiled. Along the ground, the first light snowfall sets off the green of clubmosses, especially the miniature treelike princess pines, as well as the glossy fronds of the aptly named Christmas fern. The pleasure to the eye that was afforded by the rich greenery of summer has been replaced by a quiet simplicity.

The stillness of the winter woods, if the air is calm, is likewise soothing to the senses and the spirit. Here the bustle of the human world does not intrude. Free from the tyranny of the trivia that in other settings make inaudible our guiding inner voices, we find ourselves at peace.

And this peace is not disturbed but rather accentuated by nature's own voices. Even the raucous cries of the ravens soaring overhead do not seem out of place but only authenticate the solitude that is being sought. And any hint of hostility is erased by the cheerful greeting of the chickadees that gather around the visitor and are sometimes joined in their unstudied acrobatics by nuthatches with their not un-friendly nasal notes: those of the white-breasted species confident and businesslike, and those of its red-breasted kin thin and plaintive. Or sometimes a woodpecker makes known its presence with a high-pitched, repetitive announcement accompanied by an irregular tap-ping as it searches for an insect meal in some dead limb. (Whether it is a downy or the larger and less common hairy is indicated by the rela-tive vigor of the sounds.) Even the harsh voice of the omnipresent blue jay, whose aggressive behavior at feeders is the despair of some bird lovers, is not unwelcome in this natural setting.

These are the usual avian inhabitants of the Sanctuary in winter. But on rare and memorable occasions one is made aware of transient visi-tors. Alerted by a thin, insectlike note from a nearby hemlock, one may discover a tiny bird with a greenish back, white underparts, and a yellow crown-patch flitting about in sprightly fashion. This is the golden-crowned kinglet, the smallest of our birds except for the hummingbird.

Other visitors from the north are likely to be members of the finch family. A gathering of musical twitterings from the top of a clump of conifers may betoken the presence of a flock of crossbills, so called be-cause the slender mandibles are crossed, enabling them more effi-ciently to scale the seeds from the cones of evergreens, which are their staple food. Of the two species, the more common is the red, in which the body of the male is a dark brick red, of the female a dull olive green, both with dark wings and tail. In contrast, the male of the white-winged species (which I have seen only once at High Ledges) has a body of warm pink, and the black of the wings is set off by two broad white bars. The female also has the wing bars, but the body is a modest gray-green.

In more open habitat, during a lucky winter, a sweet three-syllable whistle may call attention to a flock of pine grosbeaks, which are rela-tives of the crossbills but are more frequent visitors from the north. Both sexes resemble the white-winged species but are easily distin-guished by their larger size, longer tail, and stout beak, designed for crushing large seeds such as those of the ash, a favorite food, or, as I have observed, the seeds of wild apples.

And then there are the flocks of pine siskins, little birds with notched tails and light brown, streaked plumage, brightened somewhat by pale yellow patches on the rump and wings, whose twitterings are occasionally interspersed with a prolonged, rising buzz that makes their identity unmistakable. These birds, however, like a number of other winter species, are often lured away from High Ledges by the easier living offered at feeding stations in more populous areas.

Two other species permit their presence to be known not by their voices, unheard at this season, but by their tracks in the snow. These are the ruffed grouse with its neat line of regularly spaced three-toed tracks—the two lateral inch-long impressions at right angles to the central one of equal length—and the wild turkey, which leaves huge sprawling imprints. (Once I saw the two side by side.)

Occasionally, scanning the surface of the snow, one notes a scattering of fresh wood chips and looking up discovers a large, wedge-shaped cavity in some dead limb. This can only have been the work of a pileated woodpecker, the most spectacular member of that group—not only in color, with its starkly contrasting black and white plumage and scarlet crest, but in its size and shape, the long neck and crested head suggesting, in flight, the remembered picture of a winged dinosaur.

Less often seen than birds are the mammals that make the Sanctuary their homes, and whose presence, like that of grouse and turkeys, we

most often become aware of through their tracks in the snow. Among
the most common are those of the gray squirrel—the small imprints of
the front feet flanked by and slightly behind those of the larger hind feet,
making a neat geometrical pattern. The distance between the sets is in-
dicative of either a leisurely ramble, perhaps in search of a hidden acorn,
or a swift and purposeful passage from one tree to another. Similar but
smaller, and less often seen, are those of the red squirrel.

Both species, incidentally, are highly vocal, and the varied chatter-
ings of the gray squirrel, particularly, are among the most familiar
sounds of the winter woods.

Along the edge of the woods or in a brushy area, the tracks most frequently found are those of a cottontail as it hops about in a seemingly
aimless search for something or other. These also have the tracks of
the smaller front feet behind the larger prints of the rear feet, but instead of being side by side, like the squirrel's, one is almost directly in
front of the other. Similar in pattern but relatively enormous are those
of the snowshoe rabbit, or varying hare—"varying" because in winter
its fur changes from grayish brown to pure white. It is odd that though
I often see the tracks of showshoe rabbits, I have never caught a
glimpse of the animal itself.

This change in color to match the snow is characteristic of a crea-
ture that is perhaps a rabbit's most relentless enemy, the shorttail
weasel, whose more romantic name, in its winter coat, is ermine. Its
tracks appear in dainty pairs, giving no hint of the ferocity with which
it attacks its prey (though here, as always in viewing nature, we must
remember that moral judgments are out of place).

An equally efficient predator is one that leaves tiny prints in sets of
four, each set of which would fit inside the track of a snowshoe hare

several times. These belong to a shorttail shrew and mark its endless, ravenous search for food. Similar but larger are the tracks of the gentle white-footed mouse, whose snug nest of dry grass, lined with fur, is sometimes found in a bird box otherwise unoccupied. Less often seen are the tracks of its cousin, the meadow mouse, or vole, whose home and trails are always on the ground; sometimes after a light early snow, an elevation in the surface marks the presence of a tunnel along which the maker may pass unseen, and which a heavier snowfall will conceal completely. Only in the spring will the roofless passage be visible, winding its well-traveled way through the dead grass, often leading to a small tree whose bark has provided sustenance through the long winter. Young apple trees, if unprotected, are a favorite item in its menu.

Another bark eater, whose appetite may destroy even a large tree by stripping the upper limbs, is the porcupine, which finds a convenient den among the fallen boulders at the base of one of the many ledges on the Sanctuary. Once, on a winter day when the low western sun shone straight down one of the smaller tunnels at the Wolves' Den, I spied at the distant end a porcupine basking in the brief warmth. Its tracks in the snow are unmistakable—blurry and unpatterned, accompanied by many small parallel depressions made by the dragging tail.

Very different is the track of another forest dweller of similar size, namely the raccoon. Lured from its winter den on some warm day, it leaves a trail in which each footprint is sharply outlined, the impres-

sion of the long, slender toes suggestive of a tiny hand. And on the same warm day, especially as winter wanes, a skunk may venture forth, leaving footprints which, in sets of four, mark the corners of a parallelogram, apparently made by the feet on each side moving forward together, like those of a pacing horse.

Very different is the track of a fox—a single line of precise prints, in which the rear foot fits exactly into the impression left by the front foot like the trail of a household cat.

Of course, one is always on the lookout for the track of a deer—a neat, heart-shaped print, slender and sharp pointed if made by a doe, broader and blunt tipped if made by a mature buck. If the prints have been blurred by a thaw or are indistinguishable in deep, fluffy snow, they can still be identified by the size and the fact that, unlike a dog's, if the animal is walking, they are spaced at regular and relatively distant intervals in a single line. Of course, if it is running, the distance between the clustered sets of footprints is far greater than would be possible for any other local animal.

Along the trail one may note where the twigs of shrubs, or trees whose branches are within reach, have been browsed by passing deer. Fruit trees, especially apple, whether wild or cultivated, seem to be a favored food, but other species also suffer. Similar prunings near the surface of the snow may be done by rabbits. But the perpetrator of the damage—which is "damage," of course, only from a human viewpoint but not therefore easier to accept when done to a prized small tree or shrub—may be identified by whether the twig's remaining end is cleanly cut by a rabbit or raggedly torn off by a deer.

Trees and shrubs, now bare of leaves, also give evidence of other inhabitants of the area. A shapeless mass of dry leaves high in a tree is a gray squirrel's winter retreat; while smaller and more shapely structures are the nests in which summer-resident birds raised their broods, undetected at the time, even when near a well-traveled trail but visible in winter. A firmly woven nest in some low shrub—meadowsweet, steeplebush, or blackberry—is likely to be that of a chestnut-sided warbler. (Formerly, it might have belonged to a prairie warbler, in which case it would have been lined with brown fuzz from the stems of cinnamon or interrupted fern. Unfortunately, this species, whose presence is made known by its unique song—a series of thin notes rising in pitch almost to the limit of human hearing—and which once nested regularly at High Ledges, has been absent in recent years.)

In a similar location, a less neat nest of dry grass is that of a field sparrow, whose high, sweet, piping song in early summer evokes the essence of the season; while in a larger, dense-growing shrub nearby, a relatively bulky nest of twigs, lined with smaller fibers and leaf fragments, once contained the deep blue eggs of a gray catbird. (In former times, a similar but larger nest would have been that of a brown thrasher, whose bright brown plumage and rich song, each note once or twice repeated, cheered each summer day. But, like too many species, it is now a rare visitor at High Ledges.) In the woods, the removal of the leafy curtain may have revealed the previously unseen nest of a vireo—usually a red-eyed but sometimes a solitary—a well-woven cup, hanging from the horizontal fork of a small branch, about head high, adorned on the outside with lacy bits of white birch bark and lined with pine needles and small rootlets. This is always a delightful experience, but sometimes one is frustrated by the sight of a larger nest placed too high to permit the close inspection that would perhaps have identified the former owner.

Besides these signs of the Sanctuary's mammal and bird inhabitants, a sharp eye may discern the presence, though at this stage inanimate, of insect life. The large gray-paper nests of white-faced hornets, shaped like inverted tear-drops, now stand out among the leafless branches. Near the ground, clinging to the twigs of shrubs, one can sometimes find a smaller structure of similar gray, paperlike material—which, however, has almost the toughness of leather. This is the cocoon protecting the overwintering pupa (the stage between the larva, that is, the caterpillar, and the mature, winged insect) of one of the larger moths found in this area.

Less obvious are the eggs of other moths that pass the winter in the earliest stage of the life cycle. But there are two species—as it happens, two of the most voracious—whose egg masses are easily spotted by a practiced eye. Those of the introduced gypsy moth are light brown, fuzzy, and deposited in a roughly circular patch on the barks of trees, especially oaks, whose leaves are their favorite food. Those of the native tent caterpillar are small, tight-packed, cylindrical masses surrounding a small cherry twig—dark brown, with a shiny, lacquerlike coating.

The early Greeks—who were only beginning to engage in scientific observation leading to an understanding of nature—had many myths relating to the change of the seasons; and, in these, as might be expected, winter is often equated with death (and spring with resurrection). But the close observer of nature now knows that the appearance of death is delusive. Moreover, winter is not merely a time of rest and renewal, of passive preparation for a rebirth, but is itself a season of ongoing activity and change. Visible or invisible, audible or inaudible, vibrant or quiescent, life goes on.

CHAPTER 3

The Lure of
Ponds and Streams

I remember how, as a child, I would be fascinated in the spring by the countless rivulets born of the melting snow and the pleasure I took in scraping the mud together, with my boot, in the road or a plowed field, making miniature dams and watching the rise of the water behind them until it inevitably overflowed and washed them away. I also remember that in the wanderings that filled my summer days before I was old enough to be called on to share the farm work, I would take some simple artifact, or even some natural object like a piece of bark, and, imagining it to be a boat, follow its progress, urged by the current, along a little brook. And I remember the unreflective pleasure of watching the water bubbling up and stirring the sand at the bottom of some clear spring, or gazing at some miniature Niagara where a stream plunged over a shelf of rock. Perhaps, because life began in water, we still feel an affinity with it.

Patten Hill was where all the brooks started. Within a few hundred yards of the farm buildings were the sources of five brooks, of which three nameless streams flowed down the steep north slope to join the

North River a few miles above Shelburne Falls. The other two, Sluice Brook and Dragon Brook, descended more gradually to enter the Deerfield some miles below the Falls.

It was a matter of regret that none of them, before crossing the boundaries of the farm, became large enough to maintain a permanent flow but regularly went dry during the summer months. Hence, one of the main attractions of the streams that have carved the hills of western Massachusetts, namely brook trout, was lacking. I did, indeed, as a small boy, go fishing with my older brothers in Sluice Brook, beginning at a spring-fed pool on a neighboring farm (the "Ol' Col' Hole," of which I suppose the unabridged version would have been "Old Cold Hole"), and occasionally landed a trout that met the legal requirement of six inches in length. Through such small triumphs I came to understand the spell that angling casts upon its devotees. But I disliked threading an earthworm upon a hook (fly-fishing was unheard of in our simple world), as well as killing my catch by knocking its head against a stone (though I suppose this was more humane than letting it gradually gasp out its life). And presently, I found greater pleasure in simply watching a pool's inhabitant in its swift and graceful movement through its native element.

And in the early part of one summer, one of the brooks on the farm afforded me this delight. It flowed through the Mountain Pasture (now a part of the Sanctuary) and in a few places formed pools several feet across. In these, that summer, I was astonished and overjoyed to discover some trout not less than four or five inches long. Evidently, there had been, during the two or three preceding years, contrary to the usual weather pattern, enough rain to keep the brook running and the pools full throughout the summer.

But the real mystery was how the fish got there in the first place, since, a few hundred yards below, the brook fell over a nearly perpendicular rock face fifteen or twenty feet high, and it is impossible to imagine how an upstream-bound fish could have surmounted that obstacle. Had the eggs somehow become entangled in the feathers of a bathing bird or the fur of a wandering mammal—perhaps a mink—and then become detached at the place where I found the fish? Such a theory is almost equally defiant of the laws of probability. In the end, it must remain one of nature's mysteries—like the continuing appearance of young chestnut trees where no nuts can have fallen for more than seventy years.

At any rate, I was eager to be nature's helper in maintaining the phenomenon, and so I dammed the exit of each pool to provide more living space for its occupants. And often I would traverse the half-mile or more from the farmhouse to admire my newfound neighbors. But nature's moods are changeable and take no account of human wishes or expectations. This was to be a dry summer, and, as the days passed without bringing rain, the pools began to shrink; and presently I found them dry, with no trace of the former inhabitants.

Sometimes the brooks began in, or flowed through, swampy areas, which may once have been ponds resulting from glacial excavations. But now there was on the farm only one pool of standing water. This was in the cow pasture, about two hundred yards northwest of the farm buildings, and was called the Old Pond. It occupied a hollow between two rocky slopes, and in the spring, when it overflowed and became the source of one of the north-flowing brooks, it was about a

hundred feet long and thirty wide. During the summer, the water level declined, but there must have been a spring at the bottom, for only rarely did the shoreline retreat beyond the grass- and sedge-covered banks and hummocks. There I found it fun to search for frogs, caught by a quick grab and admired for their green backs and yellow or white throats (the colors denote, as I have since learned, not different species but different sexes of the green frog—the yellow belonging to the male, the white to the female) before being freed for a frantic dive into the safety of the muddy bottom.

Elsewhere, a grassy shore would descend gradually into shallow wa-

ter, and here there would always be some small, brown to greenish
salamanders, which I was familiar with in their juvenile, orange, red
eft form when they are terrestrial. (I then did not identify them as the
same species, red-spotted newt.) In damp weather, they make vivid
spots of color against the dark leaves of woodland trails. Or, on rare
and lucky occasions, I might spot a mud turtle, our name for a snap-
ping turtle; and, being careful to approach the right end, I would haul
it out by the tail and hold it dangling with wildly waving legs and
nothing to seize with its ample jaws.

On the Sanctuary, unfortunately, there are no natural ponds, except
for one or two vernal pools, which go dry in summer—having played
their part, however, in the life cycle of many small animate creatures.

This lack I sought to remedy by having a bulldozer hollow out a small wet area not far from the Ledges where I thought there might be a spring. My surmise proved incorrect; it was only surface water draining into the area that kept the ground wet. The work was not entirely wasted, however, for the fall rains fill the excavation each year, and, during the spring snow melt, it overflows to become the source of what I named West Brook—which flows below the Ledges and eventually makes its way to the foot of the mountain, where it turns south and, after a leisurely passage of a few hundred yards, is carried under the streets of Shelburne Falls, eventually to join the Deerfield River.

In the meantime, the pond remains full for several weeks and does not go dry until midsummer; and it becomes a favorite breeding ground for wood frogs (brown with a black mask) whose chorus of mating calls, though not musical like those of spring peepers, nevertheless provides a pleasant greeting as we approach the house on an early spring visit until they fall silent at our near presence.

But here is another instance of nature's fickle treatment of her creatures. No instinct warns the frogs that the pond is not permanent or that every year their offspring must engage in a life-or-death race to pass the tadpole stage before the water vanishes into the earth and atmosphere. The outcome depends on the amount of precipitation during the spring months; and in a season of subnormal rainfall, the shrinking pool is packed with frantically wriggling bodies whose life cycles are destined never to be completed.

Near the other end of West Brook, however, a different group of nature's creatures has worked to supply the Sanctuary with a permanent body of water. Among the species of wildlife that were nearly exterminated in the area by the European settlers was the beaver, and for more than two centuries it was absent from Massachusetts. By the 1960s—as more and more land in the western part of the state ceased to be profitable for agriculture or industry and reverted to its original state (I have read somewhere that in the middle of the nineteenth century, seventy percent of the state was clear and thirty percent forested, and that now the ratio has been reversed), and as more and more people became interested in preserving rather than merely exploiting the natural environment—the beaver staged a dramatic comeback. There was, in fact, a veritable explosion of the introduced population around High Ledges. Almost every brook in the region that flowed for even a little distance over relatively level land, especially if it crossed a swampy area, became the site of one or a number of beaver dams. At one point, the indefatigable dam builders even threatened to inundate the small wet area where the spring was located that supplied our

house with water, and a tussle ensued before I was able to frustrate their attempt.

At one site, however, I was happy with their work. This was on West Brook, where, having ended its dash down the steep slope below the Ledges—during which it descends a vertical distance of almost nine hundred feet in a surface distance of less than a mile—the brook makes its unhurried way through a swamp on the western edge of the Sanctuary. Almost overnight, it seemed, a dam appeared at the lower end of the swamp, no less than fifty yards in length, in which mud scooped up from the swamp by these small, animated bulldozers—or perhaps front-end loaders—was reinforced by the stems and branches of the alders that had once grown there. Each year the dam rose higher, and the area behind it expanded until it reached a height of seven or eight feet and the water behind it covered five or six acres.

In the meantime, the busy builders had constructed on the west shore a sturdy lodge, where during the winter they could live in comfort, subsisting on the bark of small trees and branches that they had piled on the bottom of the pond nearby. And, in this particular case, they created additional living space by excavating a number of tunnels in the sandy bank that rose steeply from the water. These, like the lodge, had underwater entrances into which the owners could retire from their surface activities, leaving human observers mystified at their failure to reappear.

At times these activities almost seemed designed to entertain an audience, since the actor, after swimming back and forth for a minute or two, would disappear with a resounding splash as it slapped the water with its thick, paddle-shaped tail, only to resurface after a moment in an unexpected location. At other times, especially toward evening, the beavers could be seen quietly feeding on the water lilies whose leaves covered the upper end of the pond.

And in the spring I could stand on top of the lodge and listen to squeaks and chirpings from below that betokened the presence of baby beavers. (Once I recorded the sounds, and after playing them to a group of friends who were birders, asked them to identify the species whose voice they were hearing.)

The pond's existence soon attracted a variety of wildlife, including two other water-loving mammals. Once, I was lucky enough to see a mink make a swift, graceful passage across the dam and along the shore; and, occasionally in recent years, tracks in the mud, or in early fallen snow before the pond was frozen over, testified to the presence of an otter.

Among the permanent residents were bullfrogs whose booming voices from the water's edge carried far across the surface; while the presence of their smaller relatives lured green-backed herons—once, at least, a great blue heron—whose squawks echoed over the water from the growth along the shore (though I never found the nest that must have been there). And, besides amphibians, they had a plenteous supply of small fish that wandered incautiously into shallow water. The fish also attracted another avian predator: a kingfisher who from some dead stub would survey the water for a likely victim of his arrowlike dive, the swift efficiency of which was in dramatic contrast to his awkward-seeming flight across the pond to another lookout, while sending forth his unique, rattling call. And once I even saw an osprey fly over, but obviously the fish were too small to attract its attention.

Other birds, transient or resident at one time or another, included a pleasantly vocal colony of red-winged blackbirds, and tree swallows that swooped over the water; and once I saw a brood of ducklings with their mother vanishing into the vegetation at the far end of the pond, too distant for positive identification. Less shy were a pair of flickers that nested in a large dead tree, one of many that were either drowned by the rising water or, too large to be felled, were girdled at the base to satisfy the beavers' insatiable appetites. In another hole—perhaps a previous home of the flickers—a pair of flying squirrels took up their residence; and if one rapped on the base, they would scramble out of the hole, about twenty feet up, scurry to the top, and launch out toward another tree that seemed to offer greater security.

More frequent observations would doubtless have made possible an even more varied and dramatic picture of this community. But it was, after all, only one feature of the Sanctuary among many that made their own claims on my time—not to mention the inescapable and even more compelling claims of the human community outside, where one is called on to be not merely an observer but an actor. Our allotted time is finite while our obligations and opportunities know no limits, or so it seems.

For no clear reason, the beavers vanished as suddenly as they had arrived. My own tentative theory is that they had exhausted the readily available food supply near their ponds.

In most cases, the water leaked out gradually through the untended dams. But on the Sanctuary, a visit to the pond soon after its abandonment revealed a huge gap through which all the water had escaped, except for a relatively small pool filling the hollow that the beavers had excavated in building their dam. There was no clear evidence as to how the gap had been created; but anybody who had ever undertaken to dismantle a beaver dam had to conclude that a human agency must have been involved—presumably with the aid of explosives.

At any rate, the pond was gone, and the passing years created in its place a "beaver meadow," supporting a rich variety of marsh-loving plants: sedges, rushes, asters, willow herbs, monkey flowers, and many others—a botanist's paradise to replace the former community of animate life forms, and, fortuitously, offering an additional resource for a friend who was writing her doctoral dissertation on the plant succession at such sites.

But this state of things proved in turn to be only temporary. On a visit one summer day toward the end of the 1980s, I noted at one side of the opening in the dam a little fresh mud holding together a few newly cut twigs and small branches. The beavers were back!

During the succeeding years, not only has the gap been filled, but along its whole length the dam has been repaired and raised to new heights, and the wildlife community that constituted one of the more dramatic features of High Ledges Wildlife Sanctuary is being reestablished.

The one unchanging attribute of nature is change itself.

CHAPTER 4

A World of Trees

Joyce Kilmer wrote: *Poems are made by fools like me,*
But only God can make a tree.

Some of my colleagues in university English departments have dispar-
aged these lines as hopelessly sentimental; as glorifying inanimate ob-
jects of nature, which have no thought or feeling, at the expense of
human beings, whose assumed unique preeminence in the world as
we know it has been given classical expression in the words of Shakespeare's Hamlet: "What a piece of work is man! how noble in reason!
how infinite in faculties! in form and moving how express and ad-
mirable! in action how like an angel! in apprehension, how like a god!
the beauty of the world, the paragon of animals!"

Leaving aside the fact that in some others of Shakespeare's plays this
ideal portrait is darkened almost beyond redemption, as well as Hamlet's conclusion—"And yet, to me, what is this quintessence of
dust?"—both sides of the argument err. The truth is that here we have
two equally miraculous manifestations of creativity, both of which
contribute immeasurably to the enrichment of human life.

People can exist, it is true, in a treeless environment. Prairies and

deserts possess their own resources to please the senses and sustain the spirit. But few New Englanders would wish to trade.

Some people may feel that their love of trees gains nothing from such analyses; they may even find them an unwelcome distraction. And they could point to a precedent in the work of England's greatest nature poet, William Wordsworth, who was happy with only an "impulse . . . from a vernal wood" and decried the intrusion of "our meddling intellect," which "misshapes the beauteous forms of things,/We murder to dissect." But to most of us, added knowledge brings added pleasure. And not the least of the many appeals that High Ledges makes to the visitor is the wealth of species of trees that cover much of the Sanctuary.

Whether people can exist without poetry is another question, to be pursued in a different context!

To be sure, all life is miraculous, animate or inanimate. But this need not diminish our reverence, if we pause to reflect, for a particular form. Can we contemplate without awe, for instance, the growth of a majestic elm, whose towering presence was once—and, we may hope, will sometime be again—a common feature of the New England landscape, from a single tiny seed? Shall we ever comprehend, however far we go in probing the genetic process, how a single cell can contain, potentially, every feature of the mature tree—the color and character of the bark and wood, the shape and texture of the leaves, the structure of the flowers, the distinctive size and silhouette when fully grown?

We need not intellectualize, of course, the unreflective pleasure with which we welcome the peaceful shade of summer woods—the tall, straight, tapering trunks supporting the leafy canopy far above— which confers a feeling of protection from possible assault by unfriendly outside forces, or at least offers a welcome respite from the wearing routine of daily life. But besides this general feeling of well-being, we may find added pleasure in the close observation of particular features of our forest world: in noting, for instance, the traits that distinguish each species from all the others. It is true that for most of us such knowledge will have no tangible value. But the Greek philosopher Aristotle spoke truly when he said that "All men desire to know"; that human beings are so made as to find pleasure in knowledge for its own sake, without regard to possible future use. We see this alike in the endless curiosity of young children concerning their immediate surroundings and in the unresting efforts of astronomers to understand how galaxies are made and move. And although this innate urge is often overborne by the practical pressures of day-by-day existence, an escape to the freedom of nature may allow it to revive.

In summer the easiest way to identify trees is by their leaves, which have a general similarity among related species and less obvious features that set off an individual species from others in the group. The leaves of maples, for instance (of which there are four species on the Sanctuary), are shaped, roughly, like a three-stubby-fingered human hand, except that the projections from the palm are sharp-pointed. But within the general pattern there are easily apparent differences. Taking the two best-known species, the leaf-edge of the sugar maple, between and along the "fingers," is smooth and unbroken, whereas that of the red maple is irregularly saw-toothed. And closer scrutiny reveals other differences, in color and texture: in the sugar maple, lighter green, thinner, smoother, and more pliant; in the red maple, darker, thicker, and stiffer.

In autumn it is the foliage of these two species that contributes most strikingly to the brilliant panorama of the New England landscape; and again we observe a pattern of similarity and difference. The leaves of the red maple begin earlier to lose the chlorophyll that conceals the latent colors, which range from clear, pale yellow through numberless shades of orange and red to a deep crimson that approaches purple; while the sugar maple, reaching its flaming climax as the leaves of its cousin begin to fall, offers a similar but narrower range, in which orange and scarlet are dominant, and which also seems, aside from the color, to have been polished by nature's touch to a brighter sheen.

In the winter, when the leaves are absent, a close inspection reveals a sharp distinction between the buds—those of the sugar maple are brown and pointed, those of the red maple, red and rounded. Or if one concentrates on the bark, which in young trees is equally smooth, one notes the buff color of the sugar maple in contrast to the silver-gray of the red maple; while in the rough-ridged trunks of mature trees, the bark of the sugar maple is broken into larger and lighter segments.

And when a tree grows in the open and can assume its natural shape, a sugar maple produces a beehive silhouette (broader and less regular after a century or so), whereas the outside of a red maple lacks this distinctive shape and symmetry.

Finally, there are the flowers and seeds. These, in all flowering plants, are to the eye of the taxonomist the primary key to classification into orders, families, genera, and species. To the nonprofessional observer, however, they are in most trees the least noticeable feature,

being usually small, dull colored, and distant from the ground. But in our two species of maple, the difference in the flowers is immediately clear. The red maple is the earliest of all common trees to blossom in the spring, the flowers opening long before the leaves and varying in color from pale to deep red; while the cream-colored clustered blossoms of the sugar maple do not appear until a week or so later. The seeds, on the other hand, differ only slightly, being attached in pairs to winged keys that eventually break apart and fall. Who has not witnessed their whirling descent, like tiny one-bladed helicopters, to the earth, where, when spring returns, they will begin a new cycle of life?

Two other members of the genus are present at High Ledges, but at first glance one may not recognize them as maples. One is the striped maple, sometimes known as "moose maple" or "moosewood," a small, short-lived tree whose trunk at maturity is only two or three inches in diameter, and whose smooth green bark is dramatically patterned by irregular narrow stripes of white. The other is called mountain maple (though in fact it usually grows in swamps) and is merely a nondescript shrub with a cluster of stems rarely exceeding an inch in diameter. But their identity as members of the genus is established by the general three-fingered shape of the leaves—those of the striped maple, incidentally, enormous and textured almost like tissue paper, those of the mountain maple similar in size and texture to those of the red maple—and by the typical pairs of winged seeds.

This essay does not aim at offering a guide to all the many northern hardwoods growing at High Ledges, but a few added notes may encourage a visitor to seek such knowledge on his own. Red and white oaks, for instance, can be distinguished at a glance by the fact that the leaf lobes of the former are pointed; of the latter, rounded. Or, in a mature woods, where the leafy crowns are far above, the white oak reveals its identity by the light, flaky bark, in contrast to the dark, deep-ridged bark of the red. And among four common birches—black, white, gray, and yellow—it is of course the color of the bark that is distinctive; though the "gray" is really a dirty white, and a second look may be needed to note the prominent black triangular patches on the trunk where there were once branches. If this fails, one can look at the small, shiny, triangular leaves. And it is also the leaves to which one must turn to identify very young specimens, when the bark is an uncertain guide. White birch leaves are larger than those of the gray; yellow and black-birch leaves are almost a perfect oval. The last two, however, are to my eye almost indistinguishable, and so I break a twig to see if it emits the strong wintergreen fragrance of black birch sap.

Or, if one is speaking of evergreens, the needles of the red pine— rarely native in Massachusetts, but dominant along the Ledges proper—are dark green, in the distance almost black, and borne in pairs; and they are almost twice as long as the paler green needles of the white pine, which grow in clusters of five. In the case of two other similar evergreens, the way to tell a small hemlock from a yew is to look at the underside of the needles and note the silvery color of the hemlock, different from the yellow-green of the yew.

In nature's original ordering of things, to be sure, the pleasure of human beings played no part; whereas to many other forms of animate life, especially birds and mammals, existence itself depends on the food and shelter supplied by trees. If one hears the word "squirrels," for instance, the automatic response is likely to be "acorns," which also help to fatten deer—and now, happily, wild turkeys—for the lean winter days ahead. Hickory nuts and beechnuts serve a similar purpose, while grouse survive the cold and snow partly on a diet of tree buds. And the cones of evergreens provide sustenance not only for squirrels but also for the several species of finches who are winter visitors from the north.

Less welcome (from our biased point of view) is the dependence of porcupines and beavers on the bark of trees, which may ultimately transform even mature specimens to stark skeletons. But we must learn not to apply *our* values to the world of nonhuman nature, and to recognize that in that realm—and in ours, too, if we face the truth—the survival of one living entity involves the destruction of others. So, most small forest-dwelling birds depend for life on the insects that in turn derive their food from trees and that, without this check, might destroy the very source of their existence.

Of course, it is not only for food that many birds and mammals depend on trees but also for shelter. Everyone has noticed, after the living leaves have fallen, a mass of dead leaves in some crotch high above the ground, assembled by a squirrel for warmth and protection. Less obvious are the natural hollows in the trunks that provide a more permanent retreat, or the holes once drilled by woodpeckers to create safe havens for their eggs and young.

Other forest birds may seek protection for their families by placing their nests high above the ground where they are less likely to be noticed by roaming predators—like the wood-pewee, whose nest of mud and fibers rests on some lofty horizontal limb. Larger birds, also, such as crows and hawks, typically seek out some tall tree and in a high crotch construct a bulky nest of twigs (though I have found a crow's nest in a relatively small white pine); and one of these may later be appropriated by a great horned owl. Smaller birds of prey, however, such as kestrels and screech-owls, prefer an interior dwelling, often the abandoned home of one of the larger woodpeckers.

And, of course, human beings in many parts of the world where trees were present and the climate called for a permanent form of shelter found wooden houses more comfortable and convenient than the cave dwellings of their ancestors.

So to the pleasure that we find in the beauty of trees, and in the knowledge of their many forms and functions, is added their usefulness, their economic value. Perhaps this is where most people's thinking about trees would start; and only a lover of poetry and a devotee of the imagination that gives it birth ("No one deserves the name of Creator," said the Italian poet Tasso, "save God and the Poet.") would find it natural to begin an essay on trees by stressing their appeal to our love of beauty and our desire for knowledge. Indeed, having worked in the small sawmill that my family acquired when I was in my teens, I still find that my appreciation of the beauty of the tall, straight, limbless trunk of some forest giant is accompanied by an estimate of the number of board feet of lumber it would produce.

But economic and esthetic values are not necessarily in conflict, for the monetary value of a species depends not only on the strength and hardness of the wood, which makes it desirable for utilitarian purposes, but also on the grain and color, which can bring beauty into our homes. Among the features that make the sugar maple my favorite tree is the hard, white, fine-grained wood that makes an uncarpeted floor or a polished piece of furniture a thing of beauty. And for the same uses I admire red oak, with its distinctive large-celled pattern and reddish tint. Similarly, the delicate grain and tone of yellow birch (which a lumber company employee once told me is the most valuable native wood) makes it the wood of choice for kitchen cabinets. But to me the most beautiful of native woods is black cherry, so fine-grained as to be almost silky to the touch, and richly toned in various soft shades of red. No exotic tropical wood, to my eye, can surpass it in beauty, whether used for paneling (as in our "dream house" at High Ledges), furniture, household utensils, or pure art in the form of sculpture.

So, however much one may have admired the living tree, one cannot regret its reincarnation in forms where use and beauty meet.

It may occur to us, here, that many former uses of wood are now served by plastics. But, practical as these may be, and even visually attractive, they do not—unless fancy misleads me—give the same pleasure as does wood to the sight and touch. We feel a subconscious affinity to something that was once alive, like us—something born of rain and sunshine, possessed of a beauty not created, but only un-veiled, by human hands.

If we lose this sense of kinship with our beginnings, with the world of nature from which we were born and of which we remain a part, our lives will be the poorer. If we look on trees as merely *things*—things to be owned and bought and sold for the sake of money, that we have a right to do with as we please—we are on the road to spiritual bankruptcy. We can agree that trees can properly be used—as they are by our fellow creatures—to provide us with homes and meet other basic needs. And some persons may dismiss as irrelevant any effort to distinguish, for praise or blame, among the motives and values involved in the conversion of a living tree to some human use. But it seems to me that one can feel a legitimate outrage at seeing a log from some great tree that has taken centuries to grow, reduced to chips that will eventually become cardboard used for cheap packaging that will in turn become part of the waste of a throwaway society—all for the sake of making a profit for some giant corporation and increasing the "gross domestic product." One is reminded of the poet Shelley's definition of obscenity as "blasphemy against the divine beauty of life."

So we return at the end of this essay to the theme with which it began, as put into words by another poet. We need not accept Kilmer's explicit formulation, but we can share his sense of the sacredness, besides all their other attributes and values, of trees.

CHAPTER 5

The Fall and Rise of the American Chestnut

Though in my childhood innocence I had no notion of the many facets of the world of trees, and found only an unreflective pleasure in their companionship as I wandered about the farm, there is one species that stands out in memory more vividly than all the rest, whose dramatic story demands a chapter of its own. This is the American chestnut.

Among the brightest memories of my early childhood is that of some blue and gold October morning when I would set out with one or more of my older brothers to "go chestnutting." Chestnut trees were common around the farm, and in early July they would be covered with thick clusters of cream-colored, yarnlike blossoms, to be followed by small, green, spiny burrs, which would grow during the next three months to spheres a little smaller than tennis balls. Then, in early October, they would split into four segments, which, opening as if on hinges, would reveal a pale, gleaming, velvety lining that offered a dramatic contrast to the harsh exterior; and inside, cushioned in a row, there would be three glossy, reddish brown nuts, whose color would later darken to that to which they lent a name.

There were potentially always three nuts, but usually only the two at the ends, or sometimes only the one in the middle, would reach a plump maturity. Tapering from a broad base to a pointed tip, they were about half the size of those sold in markets, which are imported mostly from Italy (where in season one finds the hillsides here and there softly quilted with creamy blossoms). Beneath a hard but thin covering was a crunchy nut with a distinctive flavor that a child's adventurous taste found agreeable. But only when roasted (or, less romantically, boiled) would it acquire the melting sweetness that is unique.

A few years later, my way to school was regularly "across lots" through a neighbor's pasture where there was a scattering of huge old chestnut trees, and under their spreading branches the ground in autumn would be so thickly strewn with fallen nuts that, on my way home, it would

take only a few minutes to fill my lunch box to overflowing. (I have read that in the Appalachians a century ago the nuts were so abundant that they were shipped by rail by the carload to eastern cities.)

There was, to be sure, a downside to these joys. The following summer, the dry, spiny burrs, sometimes half-hidden beneath dead leaves, would lie in wait for bare unwary feet, and the spines would all too readily transfer themselves to the flesh pressed against them. And, though so slender as to be barely visible, they pierced deep and produced a pain when pressed upon that made one willing, for relief, to endure the sharper but temporary pain of extraction by means of a firmly held needle.

A delectable but not essential addition to the human diet, the nuts were a staple food for many kinds of wildlife. Perhaps no other form of plant life contributed so much to so many of the species of mammals, from mice and squirrels to deer and bear, that inhabited the eastern forests, as well as larger birds such as jays, crows, ruffed grouse, and wild turkeys.

But to the human population, the role of the nuts as a source of food was minor compared to that of the wood, whose qualities gave it a unique value. Though it was relatively soft when green, when seasoned it took on an ironlike hardness. An old-time woodsman was quoted as saying, "Nothing dulls a crosscut saw as fast as dead chestnut." It also, though straight grained, possessed unusual tensile strength, which made it less likely than many other woods to break or splinter under stress. Add to this its almost unique resistance to decay and to insect attacks, and the reason is clear for its multitude of uses: for railroad ties and utility poles, for the sills and joists and rafters and siding of frame

buildings, and planks for the floors of barns and bridges and other structures subject to heavy use. It was also a standard wood for kitchen furniture, since, though plain grained and not richly colored, it was not unattractive and would withstand much wear and tear. Before the advent of barbed wire, it supplied the rails for fences that were easier to erect than stone walls and, though not quite so long-lasting, did not require regular "mending" or "fixing." And of course there were areas, even in New England, where stones were not available. And as firewood, dry chestnut burned with a quick, hot flame that made it ideal "sugar wood" to fuel evaporators used in making maple syrup. Finally, the bark was a main source of tannin, used in tanning hides.

The American chestnut was also set apart from many other trees by

its size. A mature tree might measure four feet in diameter at the base and eighty feet or more in height. I remember that at the family sawmill a twelve-foot chestnut log sawed out 360 board feet of lumber.

This account makes clear the immensity of the tragedy when, early in the twentieth century, the American chestnut was swiftly and, it seemed, permanently destroyed by the chestnut blight. The presence of this disease, thought to have been accidentally introduced from the Far East, was first noted in Central Park in New York City in 1904. From there it spread rapidly through the Northeast, reaching western Massachusetts about 1920.

The agent of the blight is a certain fungus whose scientific name for many years was *Endothia parasitica* but recently, through what seems to the layperson the impenetrable mystery of scientific nomenclature, has been burdened with a name as formidable as the disease itself, *Cryphonectria parasitica*. The tiny spores are spread by wind, rain, and perhaps small birds and mammals. Entering the bark through any small wound, they quickly send out a network of fine fibers called the mycelium that attacks the cambium layer (between the bark and the wood, where growth takes place) and in effect girdles the tree.

Often the first symptom of the disease is the appearance on the bark of minute orange dots, the size of small pinheads. Then, as the tree dies, a sort of brown scurf spreads over the bark, which dries and breaks open, revealing the lifeless wood beneath. All this may take place within a single year.

The effect on the foliage may be even more dramatic. One day the leaves on a branch are green and firm; the next they are pale and drooping; within a week they are crisp and brown. This may happen to the whole tree, sometimes only to the upper part, sometimes only to a single limb. But once one part of a tree has become infected, the death of the whole tree is usually only a matter of time.

This is the way the disease progresses on young, smooth-barked trees. I do not remember what visible signs, at the onset of the blight, foretold the fate of centuries-old trees with their thick, ribbed bark and massive crowns; only that, within a year or two, they would be reduced to stark skeletons.

The blight did not, however, immediately kill the roots, and new sprouts would spring up from the base of the dead trunk. But these, too, would soon be stricken, and though the cycle might be repeated several times, final surrender was, it seemed, inevitable.

Such a catastrophic blow to the timber industry naturally challenged biologists to find a way to restore the American chestnut to its original status. In this effort, scientists have pursued three lines of experimentation. (Isolated trees, here and there, have escaped the blight and have continued to produce blossoms and nuts for use in research.)

One experiment has involved crossing the American chestnut with a Chinese species that is blight resistant but whose small size make. worthless as a source of lumber. The aim, of course, was to produce hybrid that would combine the desirable properties of the American species with the resistance to blight of its Chinese relative. Although the first generation of crossings failed to achieve this goal, crossing this generation back with the original American chestnut and continuing this process has given some hope of ultimate success. This, however, is still in the future.

A second area of research involves a mild ("hypovirulent") form of the fungus that is not fatal and that inhibits the fatal action of the virulent strain. In Europe, where it was first studied, it has offered an effective check to the attack of the blight on the native species of chestnut. And, when injected into the wood of a still unblighted American chestnut (a process that one may think of as a sort of vaccination), it confers on that particular specimen immunity from the fatal strain. But no way has yet been found to make this immunity inherent in succeeding generations. Of late, however, molecular biologists have taken up the challenge and now envisage a solution to the problem through genetic engineering. But in this effort, also, success remains problematic.

In contrast to these painstaking procedures is the relatively simple hit-or-miss idea of irradiating nuts before planting them on the chance of producing a mutation that will be blight resistant and that will pass on this trait to succeeding generations. This experiment, like the others, offers some grounds for optimism, but, like them, it has not yet brought assurance of success.

So, after all these years of experimentation and research, an author-

ity could write in the July, 1990, issue of *Scientific American*, "No American chestnut tree has yet been nursed to maturity in regions infected by *C. parasitica.*"

But what do we mean by "maturity"? If we mean full growth, we are talking in terms of a century or more, and it is only ninety years since the blight first appeared on this continent. But if a tree would qualify that is ten inches in diameter at breast height and at least fifty feet tall, that has produced nuts, and that so far shows no symptoms of infection, there was such a tree on High Ledges Wildlife Sanctuary.

To be sure, this tree too eventually became infected and died, as did an even larger tree on the Sanctuary some years ago. But my personal observations during the seventy years since the blight invaded western Massachusetts suggest that nature itself, unaided, has been mounting a successful response. Although, as I have said, the sprouts that sprang from the roots of blighted trees seemed destined at first to share their parents' fate, a few persisted for a longer time and achieved a larger size before succumbing, to be replaced by others that were still more stubbornly resistant. And this process has continued.

My most dramatic success story of this kind concerns a sprout that appeared some twenty years ago near a corner of the house at High Ledges and flourished for four or five years, achieving a diameter at the base of perhaps an inch and a height of about eight feet before it was struck by the blight. But a new sprout quickly sprang from the root; I cut off the dead stem to give its successor a better chance; and the latter is now six inches in diameter and thirty feet tall, has produced blossoms and burrs, and appears to be in perfect health.

Not all new growth, however, has come from the roots of pre-existing trees. New little trees have sprung up independently where there were none before and have experienced the same process of sickness and survival that has just been described. But in the last two or three decades, there has been, at least at High Ledges, a decisive swing of the balance toward the forces of life. There are now, within fifty yards of the house, a half-dozen chestnut trees that are at least six inches in diameter and approaching thirty feet in height, besides a number of smaller ones, that as yet show no sign of infection. The fungus is still present in the area, and one notes from time to time that it has found among the smaller individuals a new victim. But so far most trees have remained immune.

There is a mystery involved in the appearance of these independent seedlings. And "seedlings" must be the proper term. There is no sign, at the place of origin, of any previous tree from whose root new life could have been derived; and this fact is confirmed in several cases by my own memory. Three years ago, for instance, a chestnut sprout emerged from the ground a few feet from the edge of the cliff—a spot where, during the sixty-odd years since I became a frequent visitor to High Ledges, no chestnut tree has ever grown. Hence, the newcomer must have sprung from a seed, a nut that perhaps some squirrel buried there before the blight. But how could a nut have lasted seventy years without decaying? And why did it wait until now to germinate? These are questions to which I find no answer.

Although it may seem from this that nature needs nothing from human beings except to be left alone, even persons who respect and revere its ways are sometimes tempted to intervene in what they see as a good cause. So when, in the fall of 1969, hiking along the side of the mountain below High Ledges, I came upon a small chestnut tree bearing some nuts (the tree died the next year), I gathered a handful and planted them, on the theory that the next generation might be less susceptible to the blight. The result was three healthy seedlings, of which I planted one at the corner of our lot in Amherst and the others at what I thought were suitable locations at High Ledges. All thrived during the early years, but the one in Amherst grew fastest and soon reached a diameter of six inches or more, and produced blossoms and burrs and even a few nuts. I collected three and planted them, but this time, for some reason, no seedlings resulted. Then the blight struck, with its swift and seemingly fatal effect. But, as usual, a new stem shot up from the base and grew vigorously for a few years, until a violent windstorm blew it down. But others immediately appeared, and one grew to a height of a dozen feet or more, and produced blossoms and burrs, but no nuts, before it died. Then it and the other sprouts were accidentally cut off but were at once replaced by others that, after one season, achieved a healthy seven feet—one of which the following year added another six feet and produced burrs, which again, however, were sterile. And though at the base of this shoot the bark shows unmistakable signs of infection, the life story of this specimen, twenty-seven years after the nut was planted, is still ongoing.

Both trees at High Ledges grew well (an additional valuable trait of the American chestnut is that it is fast-growing) and remained blight-free for about twenty years and bore, during the latter part of this period, an abundance of blossoms and burrs. Unfortunately, I did not know, when I transplanted them, that without a nearby neighbor to permit cross-pollination (by means of insects), it is only rarely that nuts mature; and I set the trees a half-mile apart! When I learned of this need, I hastened to provide each with a companion from another part of the Sanctuary, but these are still too young to serve the intended purpose. Nevertheless, in the fall of 1989, one of the original trees produced a few nuts, and from these I now have three healthy *third*-generation seedlings.

In the meantime, the parent tree, as well as its mate, recently showed symptoms of the blight. In 1989 one tree lost a limb, the next year another; and in the summer of 1991 sudden death, in the course of a week, overtook the whole upper half of the tree, to which, for months afterward, the stiffened leaves and half-grown burrs still clung. Whether, or when, the rest of the tree will die remains to be seen. As for the other tree, during the same summer of 1991, the telltale tiny orange spots appeared on the trunk and one of the larger branches fell victim to the attack.

Still, both trees have demonstrated a reluctance to surrender that contrasts with the immediate and total vulnerability of the American chestnuts that first encountered the blight seventy years ago. And if these two *do* finally die, there will be no lack of others to fill the ranks and continue the march. And though, in the normal course of things, I shall not live to see the outcome of this particular act in nature's endless drama, I am confident that it will have, from our limited human viewpoint, a happy ending.

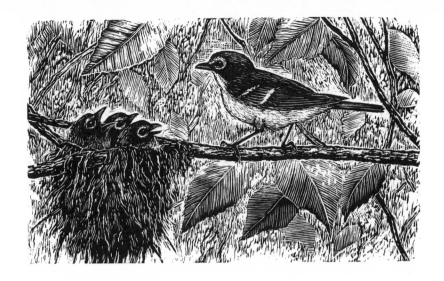

CHAPTER 6

The Life of Birds

Among the most radiant memories of my early childhood is the joy with which I welcomed the first returning bluebird in spring—a single sweet syllable drifting down from the soft blue sky, followed by a cheery warble from a nearby apple tree or fencepost.

I have often said that we do not know, ultimately, why people are what they are and do what they do. And so I have no key to the love of birds that marked my boyhood. It is true that my mother encouraged me and my three older brothers to take an interest in nature. And perhaps it was she to whom we owed the presence in our home of Chester A. Reed's *Bird Guide*, a pocket-size, paperback volume, priced at twenty-five cents, containing colored illustrations of all the species of birds in the eastern United States and Canada, together with notes about their range, their songs, and their nests and eggs. It was, I think, the first book of its kind and was surprisingly good.

Later I bought for myself from a mail-order house for $1.98 (I earned it by picking wild blueberries, which were sold to a local grocer for fifteen cents a quart) a red, clothbound volume, with a goldfinch on the front cover, titled *Birds of Eastern North America*. It was by the same author as the *Bird Guide* and contained the same material on the upper half of each page, with a running commentary on the lower half that added human interest to the technical data. I remember that I memorized, in order, the names of the five-hundred-odd species that were included. (Since then, the order has been radically changed, and I have difficulty finding the species that I am looking for.)

After my graduation from high school, my interest in birds was partially eclipsed by my involvement in college activities (and in farm work and baseball during the summer vacations), and, later, by my almost exclusive commitment in graduate school to the study of literature and philosophy. But a serious illness then led to a year of enforced leisure on the family farm; and one result was the revival, no less intense than in my youth, of my fascination with the world of birds. This stayed with me, and perhaps grew even stronger, during my years of teaching at colleges and universities in various parts of the country— Florida, New England, western New York State, and the Midwest— and vacation tours through the wide spaces of the Plains states, the Southwest, and the Far West.

Looking back, I am saddened to recall the species, familiar to my childhood, that have vanished from the hill farms—those that are left—of western Massachusetts. Among the first to go was one of my favorites, the upland sandpiper, whose prolonged, fading whistle still haunts my memory. A later departure was that of the vesper sparrow, whose rippling series of sweet, descending trills was among the commonest bird songs. Nearly gone are the eave swallows, the local name for cliff swallows, whose mud dwellings, totally enclosed except for an opening on the side, clung in rows beneath the eaves of almost every barn on the small dairy farms into which the land was then divided.

I suppose it was the color of birds that in early childhood first compelled my attention. Thoreau said that "the bluebird carries the sky on his back"; and, indeed, I know of nothing else in nature except the fringed gentian that displays a shade of blue so pure and intense as that of the male bluebird. And nothing except the cardinal flower is as brilliant a red as the body of the male scarlet tanager, set off dramatically by the glossy black of the wings and tail. And there is nothing at all to match the glowing rose-pink triangle on the breast of the rose-breasted grosbeak, in dazzling contrast to the black head and black and white wings.

My childhood encounters with the last two species—dwellers usually in the deep woods—were rare, since my summer wanderings were more often through open fields and pastures. (Now, at High Ledges, they come in early summer to eat the berries on the shad that grows a little back from the edge of the cliff, and we watch them through our living room windows.) But an everyday delight, like the bluebird, was the little goldfinch, with a body as bright as the dandelion—whose seeds, along with those of the thistle, would later provide him with food and with down to line his sturdy nest—and with black wings (barred narrowly with white) and tail, and a little black cap set perkily on his forehead.

And then, of course, there were the warblers, with colors as varied as those on a painter's palette—black, white, gray, green, blue, gold, orange, and red. In *A Hill Farm Boyhood*, I remembered "my first close view of a chestnut-sided warbler—one day in late spring, toward evening, when I was sitting in a little opening among young poplars that were taking over an unused pasture. Suddenly, among the delicate young green-gold leaves, appeared a sprightly little bird with a bright yellow crown, a grayish green back, white patches on the wings, and a white breast bordered on each side by a stripe of glowing reddish brown (too light and bright, really, to be called chestnut)."

These bright colors belong, as a rule, only to the males of the species. The females are more modestly arrayed. The blue of the female bluebird fades toward gray; the female scarlet tanager is clad in olive green with wings and tail of dull black, as is the female goldfinch; while the female grosbeak wears a demure dress like those of sparrows.

If this seems from our human perspective to be another example of life's unfairness in the treatment of the sexes, my feminist friends can argue that bright feathers are not a symbol of male dominance but only a device to win the favor of the female, who is therefore his superior. But the truth is that nature is merely being pragmatic. With most species in which the male is more brightly colored, it is the female that incubates the eggs, and it is vital that in this situation she not attract the attention of roaming predators.

The phalaropes (related to sandpipers) are an exception. In this

species it is the male who incubates the eggs and cares for the young, and it is he whose plumage is inconspicuous. His mate, whose duty is done when she has laid the eggs, sports a much more colorful costume.

No less a source of my early love of birds than the brilliance of their plumage was the beauty of their songs. The promise of renewed life that accompanies a spring dawn finds a voice in the ringing chorus with which it is greeted by a flock of robins. (Even three or four, perched among the bare branches of a nearby tree, can sound like a multitude.) Meanwhile, from a more humble station in the roadside shrubbery or the bushes bordering a field, a song sparrow sends forth his tinkling melody, simple but clear and sweet; while from a neighboring marsh or cattail-bordered pond comes the resonant far-carrying trill of a red-winged blackbird.

The red-wings are the earliest singers among returning migrants, defying the chilly winds of late winter. April brings the field sparrow with his high piping salute to longer, warmer days, and the bubbling song of the tiny ruby-crowned kinglet, poured out as if in joyous anticipation of arriving at his northern summer home. Flocks of white-throated sparrows, also on the way to their northern nesting grounds (though one or two pairs have often nested at High Ledges), pause in their rustling search for food among last year's leaves to send forth a series of prolonged, clear, whistled notes suggestive of some enchanted land. And from the still-leafless woods, the first thrush-music of the season, flutelike and ethereal, announces the return of the hermit thrush.

May welcomes the rest of the migrant throngs, and the woods and fields resound with a many-voiced chorus as a host of newcomers seek to attract mates and establish territories—although I like to think that they are simply showing their happiness to be alive. (Why should human beings assume that only *we* can feel emotions and that our fellow beings are merely driven by a blind instinct for survival?)

Some of the boldest notes are struck by those that also boast the brightest plumage, such as the tanagers and grosbeaks. Both are robin-like, clear and loud, but the former's has a hint of harshness and follows a definite pattern of five nearly identical notes, while the latter's is richer, flowing, and open-ended.

But such connections are only accidental, for another dominant woodland voice is that of the ovenbird, which seems to shout a demand for attention yet is relatively sober-suited, with upper parts of olive green and an inconspicuous, dull orange crown patch; and its ground-dwelling habits make less obvious the bold black spots on the white breast.

The songs of other warblers are mostly less flamboyant, though widely varied; some, as the name suggests, actually warble. Others have a thin and high song; yet all have in common an indefinable tone and rhythm that to a trained observer denotes their family membership. However, identifying the particular singer often presents a challenge since the same species may have two or more distinctive songs.

Warblers' chosen habitats are as varied as their voices. Some prefer deep woods, others forest borders, others bushy fields. In the last of these, chestnut-sided warblers and yellowthroats compete with sparrows, and among them all, the towhee most vigorously asserts his presence from the top of some small tree with a song that sounds like someone saying *drink your tea*. But he is sometimes challenged by a catbird, who chooses, in contrast, the concealment of a thicket from which to pour forth his endlessly varied notes. And an even louder and richer song was until recent years associated with the same habitat— that of the catbird's relative, the brown thrasher. Once common (driving in to the Ledges we would often see them dusting in the road), they are now only a memory.

People who pay only casual attention to bird songs, hearing them merely as an agreeable background blur, not only miss the full beauty of the music but also often miss the visual beauty of the bird itself, since, unless they recognize its distinctive song, its presence may pass unnoticed. Even a scarlet tanager is hard to spot in the leafy treetops where most of its life is spent.

The same unawareness—our willingness to be satisfied with only general impressions of our surroundings—leaves us largely unfamiliar

with another feature of bird life, namely, that part of the life cycle that brings into being a new generation. This has always had for me a sort of magical appeal. Almost as far back as memory goes, the discovery of a bird's nest was an experience to be treasured. I turn again to *A Hill Farm Boyhood:* "I remember my first discovery of a towhee's nest on a solitary walk through the Mountain Pasture. There was a sudden flutter beneath my feet, a quick sharp nasal note of alarm repeated at frequent intervals; and there before me on the ground, blending into the low vegetation, was a neatly woven cup containing three buffy white eggs thickly sprinkled with light brown spots, at which I gazed with an almost religious awe."

Even an inattentive observer could hardly let such almost explosive behavior pass unnoticed and not be led to seek its source. But the less dramatic departure from its nest of a smaller bird, perhaps a junco, gone almost before one can bring one's gaze into focus, and voicing its distress only by a low-volume *chip*, may fail to arrest the attention of a person not "versed in country things." And even if one's curiosity is aroused, one's patience may be exhausted before the discovery of the little nest cunningly concealed among the thick low blueberry bushes that provide a favorite habitat of this species, containing four or five off-white eggs covered with flecks of brown.

But a careful observer, alert to any sudden sound or movement, will come to an instant halt; try to determine the exact point at which the movement originated; and then, on hands and knees, with infinite care lest the nest and eggs be inadvertently crushed, scrutinize each square foot of earth and its covering vegetation. The eagerness of the search is enhanced by curiosity as to what, this time, it may reveal: perhaps a well-built cup lined with pine needles, containing three blue eggs belonging to a hermit thrush or the slightly paler ones of the veery. Or it may be the deftly woven receptacle for the eggs, typically white with a ring of darker spots around the end, of a ground-nesting warbler: perhaps a Canada, often in deep woods at the base of a ledge, or a yellowthroat, typically in more open, bushy or marshy, habitat. And once, long ago, when the species was common, I found the nest of a black-and-white warbler at the base of a large red pine a few yards back from the edge of the High Ledges proper. Most exciting of all, in those days, as I trod the leaf-carpeted forest floor, was to flush an ovenbird from its roofed-over dwelling with a small side entrance. Happily, this is one

species whose numbers have not decreased, and stumbling on a nest is not uncommon—though it never happens without a leap of the heart.

Still abundant, also, at High Ledges is another wood-warbler, the black-throated blue, whose firmly woven nest is a foot or two off the ground, typically in a bush of mountain laurel. And at a similar height, but at the woodland's edge or in an open field thickly overgrown with shrubs, is the nest of the chestnut-sided warbler, more easily found, as already noted, when winter has stripped away the curtain of leaves. Then there is the eastern wood-pewee whose nest, mostly of mud, is poised precariously on the high limb of a forest tree, and the tiny ruby-throated hummingbird, whose nest, no larger than a man's thumb, rests on a horizontal twig (in my experience, of a sugar maple) the size of a lead pencil, ten or fifteen feet above the ground and is made mostly of moss, adorned on the outside with tiny lichens and lined with vegetable down to hold the two white eggs that might pass for small, smooth, dried peas.

But, whatever the structure or location of a nest may be, the ultimate purpose, the instinctive guiding principle, is the survival of the species. Though to us the world of birds is mainly a source of pleasure, it has for many other creatures a more earthly value—that is, as a source of food. Behind the nature that we love for its beauty is another nature "red in tooth and claw," in which life and death are inextricably intertwined. Despite the most artful efforts at concealment, the most painstaking search for security, no nest is safe from one or another predator. The mortality among nests placed on or near the ground is, from our human viewpoint, tragically high. All too often, a second visit brings only a sense of desolation at the sight of an empty nest.

The list of possible predators is long—squirrels, skunks, weasels, opossums, raccoons, foxes, coyotes, and, perhaps particularly, domestic cats. Even the innocent-appearing little chipmunk has a taste for birds' eggs, as I learned when a hermit thrush's notes of distress led me, too late, to a hitherto undiscovered nest only a few yards in front of the house, where the striped marauder was busily making a meal. And then there are snakes. I remember two occasions when, letting emotion conquer reason, I intervened to remove a fledgling—one a song sparrow, one a robin—from the jaws of a black racer. The robin survived; the song sparrow did not.

To be sure, predators, also, have a right to live.

There are, of course, some species that, in nesting, seek the protection of wooden walls: the bluebird, which originally resorted to knotholes or the abandoned homes of woodpeckers but now happily accepts the homes supplied by its human admirers; the tree swallow, which competes for these dwellings and always ends its nest building with a layer of white feathers; the great crested flycatcher, whose nest also has an odd addition, a shed snakeskin hung on the outside of the nest hole; the chickadee, which typically excavates a hole in a small dead tree stub whose soft, half-rotted wood can be easily loosened (once I found a nest in the hollow top of a fence post), but will on occasion accept a little house supplied by a friendly human being to hold its six or seven white, brown-spotted eggs; and the house wren, which also raises a large family, and which, if no birdhouse is available, will resort to any kind of receptacle—once, even, an old hat on a neighbor's porch—as a container for the mass of coarse twigs behind which it tucks away its snug little nest.

Also in this group, of course, are the woodpeckers: the diminutive downy, the larger hairy, the crow-sized pileated, the yellow-bellied sapsucker, and the flicker. Their usual nesting site is a dead, but not entirely rotten, tree or limb (though the hairy is sometimes not deterred by the hardness of living wood), in which it excavates a roomy chamber floored with small chips. One may sometimes notice the nesting hole—perfectly round except for the pileated's, which is roughly triangular—placed at various heights; but the most common means of discovering a nest is the sound emitted by the young birds after they have reached a certain age, especially when they are about to be fed—a rhythmic collective utterance suggestive of a swarm of bees.

Even wooden walls, however, do not always ensure safety. Claw marks on a post supporting a bluebird house portend an empty nest, and once, in the ravaged retreat of a great crested flycatcher, I found a severed wing.

Pondering the nesting habits of birds, one is led to wonder how members of each species know where and how to build their nests. Obviously, this knowledge is not learned since a pair nesting for the first time has never observed the process, yet they follow unerringly the distinctive pattern of the species. To conclude that this pattern has somehow been built into their genes does not remove the mystery.

For some reason we find it harder to accept the genetic origin of bird behavior than of their colors and songs and, what the taxonomist considers most important, their bodily structure. Yet even for amateurs, who are concerned with identification rather than classification, the anatomy of birds is a topic of endless interest. Again, the woodpeckers offer an example. Their relatively heavy heads are set so that their long, stout, sharp-pointed bills are at right angles to the rest of the body, enabling them to drill their nesting holes as well as to dig into a tree in search of the grubs and other wood-dwelling insect larvae that constitute most of their food. The pileated makes particularly large cavities—wide enough, in one instance that I recall, to hold the nest of a robin! Another adaptation is that, whereas most birds have three of their four toes in front and one behind, most woodpeckers have two in front and two behind, the better to cling to the trunk of a tree. (Oddly, two species have only three toes—two in front and one behind.) In addition, the tail feathers are stiff and pointed, so that, pressed against the bark of a tree, they provide support while the bird hammers at the wood.

Very different is the bodily structure of nuthatches, which we associate with downy and hairy woodpeckers because all are year-round residents and are most often seen clinging to, or moving around, the trunks and limbs of trees. But nuthatches have flattened heads and bills in line with their bodies, exactly suited, as they creep up and

down or around a trunk or limb, for prying off the flakes of bark under which they find their food.

At the opposite extreme from these sturdy species, in regard to their physical structure, are the swallows and swifts, whose slender, streamlined bodies betoken the fact that they spend much of their waking existence on the wing, in pursuit of airborne insects. And since these insects are simply caught in their wide mouths, they have no need of a bill, which accordingly is reduced to a tiny knob. The feet, likewise, used so infrequently, are small and weak.

An apparent anomaly is that hummingbirds, which anatomically are close relatives of swifts, have bills half as long as their bodies for probing the depths of nectar-bearing flowers.

Other examples of these arresting instances of the vital connection ("vital" in the literal sense) between the anatomy of birds and their behavior in their struggle to survive include the slender bills of warblers, which feed almost exclusively on small insects; the short, stout bills of finches and grosbeaks, designed to crush the seeds that form much of their winter diets; and the crossed mandibles of crossbills, which are perfectly adapted for scaling from the cones of evergreens the seeds that supply their sustenance.

One wonders about the principle that has guided each bird species along its unique evolutionary path. Did the choice of a particular food supply, for instance, lead to changes in the anatomy to make that food more accessible? Or did the evolutionary process, for some unknown reason, take a particular direction and force a change in behavior in order for the species to survive?

Adding to the puzzle is the fact that some birds possess features that have no discernible relation to their survival. Of what use, for example, are the crests sported by a number of unrelated species: blue jays, cardinals, titmice, waxwings, and pileated woodpeckers? We may speculate that raising or lowering the crest indicates a change of mood, but what purpose does this serve, since most species get on perfectly well without it?

Pondering these questions, I recall the passage in Dylan Thomas's *A Child's Christmas in Wales* in which the boy receives as a Christmas gift a book telling "everything about the wasp except why." "Why?" is a question that science, for all its power as a servant (sometimes almost a master) in our "developed" society, must in the end leave to the human imagination.

From these intellectual flights, I turn to another kind of flight; the attribute of birds that, perhaps more than any other, has excited the admiration, envy, and urge to emulate, of human beings is the ability to escape unaided, defying the force of gravity, from an earthbound existence. Volumes have been written on this topic, mainly its mechanics. But for most birders the interest lies, aside from the sheer beauty of movement that some species display in flight, in its usefulness, along with the aerial silhouette, as a means of identification.

In this area, some people have a natural gift that to the rest of us seems almost miraculous. I once had a birding companion who, gesturing toward what would have been for me an otherwise unnoticed speck in the sky, would remark casually, "An accipiter at eleven o'clock." But at closer range it is not difficult to identify this genus of hawk, which includes the sharp-shinned, the Cooper's, and the northern goshawk. In ordinary flight, a series of rapid beats of the relatively short, rounded wings alternates with brief glides, while, in the darting pursuit of the smaller birds which are their prey, the long tail permits them to make sharp turns, dodging the branches of the trees or shrubs through which the intended victim seeks to make its escape.

This is in sharp contrast to the flight of buteos (our common species are the red-tailed and broad-winged) whose long, broad wings and short, wide tail are clearly evident as they circle leisurely on motionless wings high above the earth, searching, with eyes many times keener than ours, for the small animals that are their food. (A turkey vulture, which soars like the red-tail but is somewhat larger, can be distinguished by the manner in which it holds its wings in a shallow *v*, its smaller head, whose pink nakedness is only evident at relatively close range, and its longer tail.)

A third group of hawks is the falcons, including the rare peregrine whose nestings on the window ledges of skyscrapers periodically make the news, and the little kestrel, formerly called the sparrow hawk. These do not glide or soar as frequently as buteos but are propelled by the steady beat of the pointed wings.

Many species of smaller birds are less easy to identify in the air. One exception is the woodpeckers with their undulating flight; and the goldfinch, similarly, seems to bound through the air. Barn swallows sweep in graceful curves low over grassy fields; tree swallows move in circles overhead. Starlings are unmistakable, with almost triangular wings supporting chunky bodies with heavy heads and short tails; moving usually in flocks, propelled by rapid wing beats that alternate with short glides; and sometimes performing collective maneuvers with almost miraculous synchrony as members of a close-ranked flock turn sharply at nearly the same instant without colliding.

These are only a few of the most obvious examples. Although many groups have each a distinctive flight (chickadees do not fly like warblers, nor sparrows like thrushes), the difference in many instances is only discernible by a practiced birder and is difficult to describe, as if it were subliminally recorded. Still, to many persons, it is not the least of the pleasures of birding to be able to identify a bird in flight.

These categories, then—plumage, song, nesting habits, anatomy, flight—offer us a sort of guidebook through the world of birds, to which an ever greater number of human beings are turning for relief from the feverish competition for material goods and transient pleasures that these provide; and finding—in the color, the music, the mysteries of behavior, the grace of form and movement—a confirmation of our intuitive faith that life has meaning.

After completing this chapter, I was reminded of a book with the same title by Joel Welty, which covers the same topics but in much greater detail. Readers who wish more information than this chapter contains may refer to Welty's authoritative work.

C H A P T E R 7

Orchids and Asters:
Unity amid Diversity

In a previous essay, I suggested that the wealth of wildflower species from early spring (arbutus and hepatica in rare years open on the last day of March) to late autumn (once I found a fringed gentian blossom, defying the onset of winter, during the first week of November) help to make High Ledges a special place. To expand that account by merely adding particulars would soon lead to mental exhaustion in both author and reader. And yet it is the wildflowers more than any other feature that make the Sanctuary a place apart.

This essay, therefore, limits itself to two groups, offering a view that tries, within each group, to be both more intimate and more comprehensive. One is the orchid family; the other is one genus, *Aster*, of the family Asteraceae. We may think of the first as the floral elite, rare and reclusive, the other as the democratic majority, whose friendly faces greet us everywhere in late summer and fall.

To most of us the name orchid brings a mental picture of flowers of exotic shapes and colors, hanging from branches in tropical rain forests, visited by gorgeous butterflies and hummingbirds. It will therefore come as a surprise to many people that some twenty species of orchids have been found at High Ledges, ranging from the regal clan of lady's slippers to plants only a few inches high with tiny greenish blossoms, unnoticed by any but the most observant passerby.

Nearly everybody, I suppose, is familiar with the pink lady's slipper, *Cypripedium acaule.* Under the red pines along the cliff at High Ledges, it evidently finds an ideal habitat, and there, and at other places around the Sanctuary, I have counted as many as five hundred blossoming plants. But to me as a child it was a rarity, and even the discovery of a blossomless pair of the shining, deep-veined leaves brought a thrill of excitement; while the flower itself, nodding at the top of a naked, foot-high stem—the showy pink lip, in whose shape fancy may find a slipper, slanting down from what seem to be four brown petals (a technical analysis of the structure is unneeded)—stirred an emotion too profound for words.

I did not then understand the significance of the odd slit in the toe of the slipper, which, as I learned later, provides an entrance for a nectar-seeking bumblebee, after which it closes behind him, so that when ready to leave, he sees only the small opening at the base of the lip, and in forcing his way out, first brushes the pollen on his head onto the stigma to fertilize the flower and then picks up from the anthers a new load of pollen to perform the same office for the next flower that he visits.

Even earlier was my acquaintance with the much rarer yellow lady's slipper, *Cypripedium pubescens.* I cannot have been more than five or six years old when my mother took me (how did she find time, I wonder now, to leave her work as a farm housewife, in pre-appliance days, with four sons to care for?) to a place deep in the woods, beside an old logging road, at least half a mile from the farmhouse, where there were a dozen or so plants of which perhaps half had blossoms; and I still remember the wonder—almost the awe—with which I regarded them. Only two plants remain after eighty years; and other stands that I found in the same general area have vanished entirely. Happily, however, I have since found other sites on the Sanctuary (indeed, I have called one trail the Lady's Slipper Trail), and the latest census tallied 140 flowering plants—some with two blossoms.

The flower of the pink species is always solitary, and the two also differ in their choice of habitat. The pink one prefers the presence of evergreens and thrives in dry soil (though it is sometimes found along the edges of swamps), whereas the yellow one chooses moist deciduous woods, sometimes even wooded swamps. But it is in appearance that the two differ most dramatically. The leaves of the yellow species, instead of being paired at the base, are borne upward along the stem, alternately, becoming a little smaller toward the top, and lack the sheen of its pink relative; and the glowing golden lip of the yellow species really *is* shaped like a slipper, with a broad, rounded toe and the opening is at the top, where it *should* be; and the brown petals at the base are longer and more slender and have a charming twist.

It is hard to understand what principle—Darwin's or another— could have guided the evolution of an organism so intricately designed (though not more so, I suppose, leaving aside the esthetic taste with which *our* evolution has endowed us, than any common weed!). Indeed, such phenomena seem to me (barring revelation, which is only valid to the person to whom it has been granted) the strongest evidence that the natural world is the work of a Divine Intelligence. But religious faith does not depend on physical facts, and I myself am only able to acknowledge the presence of a mystery.

I may have been about ten years old when, in my wanderings about the farm, I discovered an orchid species new to me. By this time I had become interested in flowers in general, encouraged by the Reed *Flower Guide,* a companion to his *Bird Guide* and possessing the same virtues. Though it did not command such eager attention as the latter, it made me aware that there were groups of related species, and that lady's slippers were not the only members of the orchid family.

There was, however, little evidence of a family relationship between them and my new discovery, the showy orchid, *Galearis spectabilis.* Contrary to what its name suggests, its beauty is delicate rather than dramatic. The three or four pink-hooded, white-lipped blossoms (sometimes the lip is also pink) are borne on a stem only a few inches high, rising unobtrusively from a pair of basal leaves much smaller than those of the pink lady's slipper, more nearly oval and rounded instead of pointed at the end, and perfectly smooth and glossy rather than deeply veined.

Its beauty is enhanced by its rarity. It is now long absent from the place where I first found it, and I know of only one small area on the Sanctuary, along the Lady's Slipper Trail, where it occurs. It has the puzzling habit, like some other orchids, of disappearing from a particular location and reappearing some years later in the same area; more often, the departure is permanent, but in another, distant, location, it may make an unpredictable appearance.

This phenomenon is perhaps related to another distinctive family trait. The seeds are almost microscopic, and so I suppose may be windborne for a considerable distance; and they will only germinate in the presence of a particular microorganism, a process that may take several years. Still, there is something mysterious about the appearance of a species as if from nowhere and, after a few years, its equally sudden, unexplained departure.

The same small area where I can now expect to find the showy orchid is home to another rare member of the family, Hooker's orchid, *Platanthera hookeri*. The leaves are not dissimilar to those of the last species, though they are perfectly oval and lie flat on the ground; but the leafless stem, averaging eight to ten inches in height, ends in a spike of many tiny, close-set, long-spurred flowers with a lip of pale yellowish green.

In the same location, a few years ago, two plants of the long-bracted orchid, *Coeloglossum viridis,* made their appearance. Instead of the two broad basal leaves, this species has two or three narrow leaves along the six-inch stem, growing smaller toward the top and vanishing into a loose raceme of a few small, plain, green flowers. A rare and transient dweller on the Sanctuary, it has now vanished from this site, as it has from other areas where I have occasionally found it in previous years. But one may reasonably hope that it will eventually show itself in a different place. Or perhaps it is already there, waiting to be discovered.

Following the same unpredictable pattern, but even rarer, is the round-leafed orchid, *Orbiculata macrophylla.* I had never seen one until the spring of 1979, when a member of a tour group on the way to the Gentian Swamp noticed, a few feet off the trail, a pair of huge leaves lying flat on the ground, like those of a Hooker's orchid but perfectly round and five or six inches in diameter. The top of the stem was missing (perhaps eaten by a deer), but the leaves made the identification easy. And the following year the flowers were present, in a spectacular cylindrical raceme two inches or more in diameter and perhaps three times as long, composed of many loosely set cream-colored flowers not less than a half-inch wide, with inch-long spurs.

This plant flourished a few years and then died, as did a smaller one nearby that never reached the blossoming stage. But presently another plant made its appearance a half-mile away, just north of the Spring Area, and then another a hundred yards to the south, beside the Waterthrush Trail. Both bloomed for a few years and then vanished. But one may hope that at some future time a lucky wanderer about the Sanctuary will come upon a pair of huge, round, shining leaves, green against the brown forest floor.

Between this period and my earliest acquaintance with our native orchids, there were many other meetings with new species, and the eagerness with which I welcomed each is still fresh in my memory. It may have been two or three years after my discovery of the showy orchids that the next encounter occurred. One day on a midsummer ramble, crossing the Big Swamp—an open marsh perhaps an acre and a half in extent, fed by a small brook that went dry in summer but also by a spring that never failed—I was brought to a sudden halt by an unfamiliar and enchanting sight. Standing out against a neutral tone of the marsh grasses and sedges was a magenta pink cylinder composed of densely packed, delicate, small flowers with fringed lips, topping a knee-high stem (knee-high to a boy of twelve, that is) on which the elongated shining leaves, placed alternately, grew smaller as they approached the crowning mass of bloom.

This, I learned from the *Flower Guide,* was a small purple fringed orchid, *Platanthera psychodes* (celebrated by Robert Frost in "The Quest for the Purple-fringed"). Later I would find it in other areas that are now included in the Sanctuary; and, indeed, it is one of the species that led to the naming of the Orchid Swamp. The original location, unfortunately, was flooded by beavers during the population explosion of the sixties and seventies. Had I learned of this event sooner, I should have tried to rescue some of the plants, but when I discovered what was taking place, the rising water had already covered them.

The Orchid Swamp is also the home of the large purple fringed orchids, *Platanthera grandiflora,* whose raceme contains fewer but much larger blossoms than its smaller relative. It is also much rarer and indeed is in danger of disappearing from the Sanctuary altogether. One threat comes, I think, from deer, which I suspect have been guilty of browsing off the flowers—once, on both of the small stands with which I am familiar. (I attribute to deer, also, a fondness for yellow lady's slippers, Canada lilies, and other handsome species—a taste that tests the admiration and affection created by the animals' beauty and grace! But this is nature's way.) I have no explanation for its disappearance from the spring area, where two or three plants once grew and blossomed.

At the edge of the Orchid Swamp, close to the few remaining plants of the species just discussed, there is a thriving stand of small green wood orchid, *Platanthera clavellata.* One might easily overlook it, however, for the slender stem is only a few inches high, with a single small leaf an inch or so above the base and a cluster of only four or five tiny, cream-colored flowers—not without appeal, however, on a closer view. Fortunately, unlike many of its relatives, it has shown, in this location, no decline in numbers.

The Orchid Swamp is also the home of the northern green orchid, *Platanthera hyperborea* variety *huronensis.* Of all the orchids at High Ledges, this has, for me, the least esthetic appeal, even though it is the tallest native member of the family, reaching a height of as much as thirty inches. But the relatively narrow leaves along the straight, stiff stem are not proportional to the height, and the terminal spike of small, tight-set, dull green flowers is even more disappointing. It is uniquely interesting, however, in that the typical form of the species, which has been found at several places on the Sanctuary, may be only a few inches tall. In fact, for a time, I tentatively identified it as a different species before finally accepting the verdict of the authorities that the tallest and smallest of our orchids are members of the same species, identical except in size.

An odd fact about the smaller form is that I once found several albino plants, completely devoid of chlorophyll. How they survived, I do not know, but they were present for several years before taking leave in typical orchid fashion.

Most orchids choose a woodland habitat, but there is one species, the ragged fringed orchid, *Platanthera lacera,* that shuns the shade and is found only in areas open to the sky and, again unlike most members of the family, in dry as well as in moist soils. In form it might at first be taken as a variant of the small purple fringed orchid (of which I once found a specimen with pure white flowers), but the greenish white lip is deeply and irregularly cut. Like many of its relatives, it is peripatetic, making unpredictable arrivals and departures in one or another of the Sanctuary's open spaces. (One year a specimen showed up in our yard in Amherst—I have never seen one elsewhere in the town—and, a year or two later, another joined the inhabitants of a small wildflower garden only a few feet from the foundation of the house. Both proved to be transient visitors.)

One orchid species I stumbled on only a few years ago in a small, shaded, swampy area near the northwestern corner of the Sanctuary. (It was named, by a friend who did a biological census of High Ledges, the Violet Seep.) Always on the lookout for new species, I noted among the surrounding vegetation a pair of unmistakable orchid leaves, similar to but smaller than those of the showy orchid. Further searching revealed three other plants; but the flowers had fallen from

the slender stems, only inches high, and I could not be sure of the identity. The following year, however, I sought it out at an earlier date, and found it in blossom. Not knowing what to expect, but hoping for something colorful and strange, I was disappointed by the three or four minute greenish flowers, which identified it as bog twayblade, *Liparis loeseli*—surely among the least conspicuous of our native orchids. Still, it is one more species to be added to the list. And happily, the four plants have persisted.

Another orchid, helleborine, *Epipactis helleborine,* is an immigrant from Europe that was not present during my boyhood but is now common in wooded areas about the Sanctuary. Its stem and leaves suggest a smaller version of the yellow lady's slipper, but it has a raceme of small, close-set flowers varying in color from pale green to pink. At a distance it offers a sort of nondescript appearance, unapt to invite a second glance; but I have a close-up slide of a single flower that approaches our mental picture of a rich-toned dweller in the tropics.

The list grows long, but each new genus and species offers new and often delightful features. Among these are the ladies' tresses, genus *Spiranthes,* of which the common species, nodding ladies' tresses, *Spiranthes cernua,* is as charming as its name. It is a small plant growing in moist, sunny places, with grasslike leaves mounting a slender stem

that bears a multitude of small white flowers. The petals of each are fused into a tiny tube, the delicate open end hooded and with a minute lip (in which a discerning eye may detect a relationship with other members of the orchid family); and all the little flowers are arranged in a distinct, slightly spiral row suggestive of a braid of hair.

A less common member of the genus—in fact, I have found it only once, beside the road leading in to the Ledges, in a very dry area—is the slender ladies' tresses, *Spiranthes lacera* variety *gracilis,* whose slender stem, nearly a foot in height, rises from a basal rosette of leaves and bears a single row of minute white flowers spiraling gracefully upward. Unhappily, this group of half a dozen plants, having appeared as if from nowhere, vanished a few years later with equal suddenness.

Emulating the growth pattern of the previous species are the members of another genus, *Goodyera,* commonly known as rattlesnake plantain. (Why "rattlesnake" and why "plantain," I do not know.) The handsomest member of the group, and the most common, is the downy rattlesnake plantain, *Goodyera pubescens,* whose gray-green leaves, in a rosette at the base of the stem, are dramatically veined in white, but whose tiny white flowers, forming a close-knit raceme along the upper part of the six- or eight-inch stem, require a magnifying glass to fully reveal their delicate beauty.

Two other members of the genus have also found a home on the Sanctuary: checkered rattlesnake plantain, *Goodyera tesselata,* much like the previous species except that the leaf-veins are dull white and so less striking; and dwarf rattlesnake plantain, *Goodyera repens,* distinguished not only by the small size but by the fact that the flowers are all borne on the same side of the stem. It is known to grow in only one other place in Massachusetts.

The final genus, *Corallorhiza,* the coral-roots, adds yet another face to the family portrait. Its members are saprophytes, plants that have lost their chlorophyll and draw their nourishment from decaying organic matter in the soil, and whose leaves, no longer needed, have been reduced to mere scales. The most familiar example is Indian pipe, which of course is not an orchid. The coral-roots are much less common, but two members of the genus may be found occasionally at High Ledges: northern coral-root, *Corallorhiza trifida,* growing in wet woodland areas, with a pale yellow stem that bears, in mid-May, a raceme of tiny white-lipped flowers; and spotted coral-root, *Corallorhiza maculata,* which has a taller stem of reddish brown shading toward purple, whose flowers have spots of the same color on the white lip, and which blooms in late summer.

Other species of orchids are native to western Massachusetts, and it

may be that some remain to be discovered at High Ledges or may at some future date make an unexplained appearance. But this account shows what a rich variety of species of this mainly tropical family have been able to adapt to the chaste climate of New England. What brings together all the members of the family, despite their spectacular differences in size, color, and form, is primarily the structure of the flowers. This is a matter for a professional botanist, armed not merely with a magnifying glass but with a microscope. Though I think I have acquired a *feeling* about orchids native to the area (the ability, for instance, to distinguish at a glance between the leaf of an orchid and that of *Clintonia*, which belongs to the lily family), the only obvious common feature is that one petal has evolved into a "lip," which, though varying in form and color, is always at the front of the flower and below the strictly reproductive parts, the stamens and the pistil. And of course there are members of other families that are superficially similar in this respect.

In the Asteraceae the differences among the many genera are at least as great as those in the Orchidaceae. Who would expect, for instance, to find dandelions and ragweed in the same family? But there is one genus, *Aster*, in which the essential structure of the flowers, the defining characteristics of the family, are clearly present. And yet, even here, the uninitiated can be led astray. What look like petals are, or were at an earlier stage of evolution, each a complete flower, which now has lost its reproductive parts and taken on the limited function of attracting insects to pollinate the tiny fertile flowers massed within the circle of pseudopetals. These flowers have become specialized in their

own way, the fused petals having shrunk to almost nothing, surrounding an ovary that will ultimately produce a single seed.

Given the common structure of their flowers, however, even the members of this one genus are almost as varied as orchids—in size, in color, in leaf shape, in habit of growth, in choice of habitat.

Perhaps to many persons the genus name suggests the New England aster, *Aster novae-angliae,* whose masses of purple or pink inch-wide blossoms at the top of tall, leafy stems brighten many an abandoned meadow. Less colorful but somewhat similar in its manner of growth—a tall main stem with many narrow, pointed, stemless (the technical term is "sessile") leaves, similar in size from the base to the crowning mass of flowers (for convenience I will use "flower" for the whole flower-head)—is the flat-topped aster, *Aster umbellatus.* But the leaves are glossy rather than dull green, the flowers are a little smaller and less impressively massed, and are arranged, as the popular name suggests, in approximately the same plane.

In this respect it differs from another tall, leafy-stemmed species, panicled aster, *Aster simplex,* whose wide white flowers open at the ends of longer branches so that they are less closely packed and each has an individual identity and grace.

Very different is another typical growth pattern—a many branched and wide-spreading stem with the slender, tapering leaves becoming smaller as they approach the flowering tip of each branchlet. Most conspicuous in this group is the purple-stemmed aster, *Aster puniceus,* rising almost head high in swamps, beside slow-flowing brooks, or in damp ditches along country roads, whose stem usually—not always—

is dark reddish purple, and whose branches end in wide-eyed blossoms of light blue.

Two other species conforming to the same pattern of growth but drawn to a smaller scale, are the calico aster, *Aster lateriflorus,* and small white aster, *Aster vimineus.* Both have many tiny flowers, sometimes not more than a quarter-inch across, borne close together along each branchlet toward the end; but the many white ray-florets of the former have just a hint of lilac and encircle a purple center, while the florets of the latter are pure white around a yellow center and are even more crowded.

Other species conform to a third pattern: one main stem, a foot or two high, branching only toward the top; the usually heart-shaped leaves borne on stems, or petioles, large at the base of the plant and gradually diminishing in size; the flowers about half an inch across, blue or white, and loosely clustered.

Here we find the large-leaved aster, *Aster macrophyllus.* (I sometimes find it hard to remember whether "large-leaved" translates the Greek, as it does here, or the Latin, *grandifolius.)* The leaves are indeed impressive, spreading in dense mats, usually in lightly shaded areas.

But only a relatively few plants produce flowers, and these I have always found a little disappointing since the flowers are few, and the sparseness of the pale blue rays conveys, to me, a sense of incompleteness.

The most common member of the group is the white woodland aster, *Aster divaricatus,* which grows only in woods or shaded areas, whose leaves are deeply and irregularly toothed, and whose white flowers, in early fall, may suggest a high-piled carpet spread along the forest floor. Sometimes in open woods they have for neighbors two other members of the genus: heart-leaved aster, *Aster cordifolius,* and the wavy-leaved aster, *Aster undulatus;* but, as a rule, these blue-flowered species are lovers of the sun, and—the latter, especially—massed along the borders of open fields or on unmown roadsides, blend happily with other features of the landscape. I find the two flowers indistinguishable; but the leaves of *Aster undulatus* are indeed wavy rather than toothed, are narrower, especially toward the top, and have winged petioles (that is, the stems have become widened and leaflike); and sometimes toward the end of the season they take on a purple hue.

Finally, there is the whorled aster, *Aster acuminatus,* whose stemless, pointed leaves are gathered in a whorl below the loosely clustered flowers, and whose long-stemmed, drooping, dull white blossoms present, to my eye, a somewhat ragged and unkempt appearance, contrasting sharply with the trim floral outlines that generally mark the genus.

As is true of the orchids, there may be other asters at High Ledges, for the genus has many members, some distinguished by only slight differences; and a certain identification of every species that occurs in western Massachusetts requires more knowledge than I possess.

These two groups of wildflowers, orchids and asters, comprise a reluctant selection from the whole flora of High Ledges Wildlife Sanctuary, whose infinite variety and beauty deserve a whole book. But perhaps the intimate treatment accorded them (hopefully not wearisome in its details) will emphasize, again, a constant theme of these essays: the way in which our knowledge of nature is expanded and our lives accordingly enriched if we stop to take a closer look at the natural world around us than, in the ceaseless rush of daily life, we usually think we have time for. The poet Shelley speaks (echoing Coleridge) of "the film of familiarity which obscures from us the wonder of our being." But the "familiarity" that he refers to is unthinking and unobservant; and the implied alternative, which informs the present context, is a different kind of familiarity, loving and attentive, that intensifies rather than blurs our awareness of the wonders of the natural world.

One of these wonders is the presence of unity in diversity—for example, the common underlying structure of the spectacular lady's slippers in contrast to the seeming near-nonentity of some small, green species of another orchid genus—where there is hardly a hint of such a relationship; or, to put it differently, the presence in nature of a principle or order that binds together a confusing multiplicity of forms lets us think of ourselves as inhabitants of a world that is at least partially intelligible.

Pondering these ideas, and reflecting that we, too, are a part of nature, we may come to realize that, despite differences in such physical traits as the color of our skin or the shape of our facial features, and despite differences in social traits such as language, customs, and beliefs, we all belong to a single species. Every trait that goes into the definition of "human" is a trait that we all possess. The implications of this unity, if we were willing to acknowledge it, would change the world.

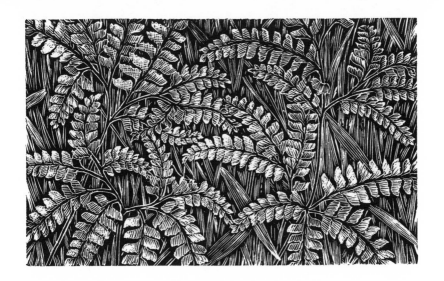

CHAPTER 8

Plants without Flowers

When winter's approach is announced by somber skies and shortening days, by the sweep of chill winds through skeleton woods, and by the ground's dull carpet of dead leaves and frost-stricken flowers, one form of plant life defies the change of seasons and marches with its green banners across the brown earth.

This cheerful army is composed of clubmosses, intermediate in evolutionary status between mosses and ferns. They reproduce not by seeds but by spores—so minute, I learn from a friend who is a physicist, that they are used in certain industrial processes that call for smaller particles than can be artificially produced—so small that at a certain season, when the spore-bearing stalks are disturbed, they release a cloud of what looks like pale yellow smoke.

Of the four species found at High Ledges, no doubt the most familiar is *Lycopodium obscurum,* popularly called tree clubmoss or princess pine, which does, indeed, look like a miniature pine tree. What looks like an individual plant, however, is actually an erect branch of a horizontal underground stem, part of a network from which other branches arise to form a lilliputian forest. When I was a child, innocently assuming that nature's resources were inexhaustible (except for a few rare species of flowers), I joined my schoolmates in

using this species to make Christmas wreaths, pulling up plants by the dozen, tying them into small bunches, and then binding these tightly together to form a solid wreath.

In other species, the main stem lies along the surface of the ground, making the vinelike growth apparent. One of these is *Lycopodium complanatum,* known by several common names including ground pine, ground cedar, and running pine. In this species, the erect branch is crowned by a flat, horseshoe-shaped cluster of horizontal branches. Another creeping form is *Lycopodium clavatum,* staghorn clubmoss, which has no vertical branches; instead, the main stem is forked, and each fork, as it creeps along the ground, divides again, producing a thick mass of branches, of which the outer ends may be thought to look not only like the tips of a stag's antlers but also like the claws of a wolf; and this appearance perhaps gave rise to the genus name, which may be translated as "wolf foot." The light, bright green color of the branches and the furry look created by the tiny needlelike leaves make it, to my eye, the handsomest member of the genus.

This and the previous species were also suitable for Christmas wreaths, formed—much less laboriously—by taking a slender, pliant branch of a tree or shrub, tying the ends together to form a loop and winding them with the long, trailing evergreen stems and branches.

Somewhat similar to staghorn clubmoss is shining clubmoss, *Huperzia lucidula;* but the stems do not fork or spread as widely, and the "leaves" are longer, suggesting, to a lively imagination, the spines of a

long, fuzzy, dark green caterpillar lifting its head to view its surroundings. Unlike the other three clubmosses, which lend their charm to open woods or untended fields, this one thrives only in deep shade, often beside a mossy boulder.

Like the clubmosses, ferns also lack flowers and reproduce by means of spores, but they form a much larger and more varied group, of which High Ledges is host to some thirty species, adding to the visual richness of the green woodland world through which one moves along the trails or, less commonly, lending variety to the vegetation of open fields or forest borders.

Perhaps to the casual glance of the uninitiated, ferns are only ferns, undefined green shapes in clusters or masses here and there, forming an undistinguished part of the summer landscape. One of the most familiar is the hay-scented fern, *Dennstaedtia punctilobula*, which, when crushed, emits a fragrance thought by some to resemble that of new-dried hay. (Readers may choose to skip the scientific names, whose pronunciation, difficult at best, is made still more uncertain by the arbitrary use by different persons of ancient Latin or modern English vowel sounds. But the genus name, especially, may indicate unsuspected relationships, or, on the other hand, establish distinctions between species whose superficial forms or popular names may be misleading.)

As this species begins to reclaim for nature fields no longer devoted to the production of real hay, it offers a general impression pleasing to the eye. But a closer look reveals a number of particular characteristics; and it is by such characteristics that relationships and distinctions are established among families, genera, and species.

As in flowering plants, it is the structure of the reproductive parts that is the most important in classification, often involving the use of a magnifying glass, or even a microscope. But, for the amateur observer, most common species can be identified by more obvious features. The leaf, or frond, may vary in length and height among different species, from a few inches to several feet—from ankle high to head high (though there may also be great variations in size among individuals of the same species); it may be plumelike, erect or curving, or roughly triangular, at the top of a more or less vertical stem; it may be solitary, from a spreading underground rootstock, or one of several gathered around a solid center; it may be filmy or leathery in texture; it may be divided and subdivided in various ways; the spores may be borne on the underside of the branchlets of the green frond, or on a separate stalk; and almost every species displays a different shade of green.

Hay-scented ferns, for instance, conform to the most common growth pattern—a central stem (solitary in this instance), at first rising vertically and then curving gracefully outward, with close-set lateral leaflike branches called pinnae, relatively short on the lower part of the stem, lengthening toward the middle, and then decreasing to end in a point. Each pinna, in turn, repeats the original pattern, producing its own lateral branches, called pinnules, whose edges are sometimes, as in this species, toothed so as to suggest a still further division.

Another defining trait of this species, shared by many but not all others, is that the spores are borne on the underside of the pinnules, clustered together in tiny "fruit dots." This is also true of the lady fern, *Athyrium filix-femina*, whose clustered fronds, larger and darker green than those of the hay-scented fern but no less delicate in detail, lend their grace to any lightly shaded area. Its relative, silvery spleenwort,

Diplazium acrostichoides (unfortunately named, since the true spleen-worts belong to an entirely different group), thrives in wet woodland places, differing from the lady fern in that the pinnules are smooth edged ("entire" in technical language) rather than toothed.

These particular traits—the structure of the fronds and the location of the spores—are shared by a large group of ferns whose genus name, *Dryopteris*, suggests their woodland habitat. In Greek mythology, which often gives human attributes to natural forms and forces, dryads were nymphs whose existence was identified with trees—as na-iads with springs and streams, oreads with mountains. Most beautiful, to my eye, are the filmy, feathery fronds of the spinulose wood fern, *Dryopteris carthusiana*, though the dark green, firm-textured fronds of the marginal wood fern, *Dryopteris marginalis*, lend great charm to the boulders and ledges whose presence they always seek.

An entirely different environment is favored by the crested fern, *Dryopteris cristata*, which is never found except in swamps. The fronds have the same rough-appearing surface and leathery texture as those of marginal wood fern but are narrower, taller, and more erect. (A larger form with wider fronds, sometimes treated as a separate species, is Clinton's wood fern, *Dryopteris clintoniana*.) And along the margins of the same swamps one may, with luck, encounter the rare and stately Goldie's fern, *Dryopteris goldiana*, whose wide, curving fronds have pinnae that at the base are a deep bluish green but toward the tips take on a tinge of yellow.

Also favoring moist soils, but, like the hay-scented fern and unlike most others, preferring sun to shade, is the marsh fern, *Thelypteris palustris* variety *pubescens*. Rather small, with a somewhat narrow frond in which both the pinnae and pinnules are more widely spaced than usual, giving it a more or less open appearance, it is a species that is easily taken for granted, as is its relative, the New York fern, *The-lypteris noveboracensis*—partly because the latter is the most abundant of all woodland ferns. It is easily identified by the fact that the pinnae become progressively smaller toward the base of the stem until they simply peter out.

Very different in shape, though formerly placed in the same genus,

are the two beech ferns—the long beech fern, *Phegopteris connectilis,*
and the broad beech fern, *Phegopteris hexagonoptera.* Each has a
smooth, slender stalk—several inches high in the former, typically a
foot or so in the latter—ending at the base of a leafy triangle that
spreads almost horizontally. Otherwise, they differ both in form and
habitat. The broad species offers to the view an almost equilateral triangle and seems to prefer relatively open woods, while the smaller and
narrower fronds of its relative have the first two pinnae bent sharply
backward and are typically found in close-growing groups along
shaded brooks, like patches of dark green carpet.

The triangular shape of the frond is shared by a number of other
species, including two that in other respects could hardly be more different: the large, coarse brake fern, or bracken, *Pteridium aquilinum,*
two feet tall or more, aggressive in taking over dry, barren, open areas;
and the rare and delicate oak fern, *Gymnocarpon dryopteris,* whose
filmy fronds, only inches high and broad, rise on smooth black stems,
threadlike in thickness, from moist soil in shaded locations.

Also marked by the triangular shape of the frond are members of a
group only distantly related, called grape ferns, belonging to the genus
Botrychium. The most common and visible of these is the rattlesnake
fern, *Botrychium virginianum,* found in moist woods, whose lacy triangle crowns a green stem about a foot high; and from the center of

this triangle rises another stem supporting a mass of spore-bearing elements.

The general shape of the frond is the only obvious link to two other members of the genus: the leathery grape fern, *Botrychium multifidum,* and the cut-leaved grape fern, *Botrychium dissectum.* Their variant forms are not always easy to tell apart, having fronds that are not only darker in color and fleshier in texture than those of the rattlesnake fern but also are so small and low growing as to be often hidden by the grasses, herbs, and low shrubs among which they are found in open or lightly shaded environments. Their frequently accidental

discovery is always a pleasant surprise. Moreover, the spore-bearing stalk grows independently from the base of the green frond.

Still less recognizable as a member of the genus is the daisy-leaf moonwort, whose tongue-twisting scientific appellation is *Botrychium matricariifolium.* The tiny triangular leaf, less than an inch broad, is borne on one side of a slender stem halfway up to the minute terminal cluster of spore-bearing elements. Luck and a sharp eye are both necessary to detect its presence.

Less symmetrical but still generally triangular is the frond of the sensitive fern, *Onoclea sensibilis.* Common along roadsides and in wet waste places, it lifts its light green fronds a foot or two above the ground and is immediately identifiable by the fact that the pinnae, instead of being divided into pinnules, are simply scalloped along the edges. "Sensitive," incidentally, refers to temperature. One may have observed, after a late spring frost, a marshy area black with the lifeless fronds.

One identifying trait of this species, shared with the grape ferns and others, is that the spores, instead of being located on the underside of the pinnules, are borne on a separate part of the plant, usually an independent stalk. In the case of the sensitive fern, this stalk is still present, dry, dark, and rigid, the following year.

A similar structure is a feature of the ostrich fern, *Matteuccia struthiopteris* (a layperson may wonder why scientists are apparently so addicted to linguistic gymnastics). This is one of the largest, and certainly one of the handsomest, of all our ferns, whose popular name suggests the gracefully curving plumes rising in symmetrical order from a common base, widening outward before rounding to a point (and sharing only with the much smaller New York fern, the feature that the pinnae grow progressively shorter toward the base until they finally disappear). This is the species, incidentally, whose fronds in their emergent state are the "fiddleheads" sold in markets as a gourmet food—a sacrifice of visual beauty to physical appetite that in my view is scarcely less than blasphemous!

The most familiar fiddleheads, however, are those of the cinnamon and interrupted ferns, *Osmunda cinnamomea* and *Osmunda claytoniana*—light green, fuzzy, solid, almost aggressive in the upward thrust of the close-clustered stems, aiming toward a height, at maturity, of six feet or more. (In the Orchid Swamp, the cinnamon ferns are in some places so tall and dense as to form a veritable jungle in which I once actually got lost!) The green fronds of the two species are almost indistinguishable; only a close inspection reveals that the green of the interrupted species is a shade darker, the pinnules more closely spaced, and the ends of the fronds rounded rather than tapered to a point. But when they have reached the spore-bearing stage, one may wonder whether they really belong in the same genus. The cinnamon sends up, along with the green fronds, a cluster of sturdy stalks supporting solid masses of spore-bearing elements—black at first, then

brilliant light reddish brown, presently drooping and collapsing. In contrast, the spore-bearing parts of the interrupted species occur in the middle of the otherwise green frond, the obvious source of the common name.

The third member of the genus, the royal fern, *Osmunda regalis,* would hardly be recognized as the relative of the other two. Both the pinnae and the pinnules are so large and widely spaced as to produce a sort of network effect. And though the fertile elements are, as in the interrupted fern, borne on the same frond as the sterile green parts, they are located at the end rather than in the middle. But these differences do not diminish its attractiveness; and, in the alder swamps that are a favorite habitat, it achieves a stature that does, indeed, justify the name.

Superficially similar in the location of the spores is the Christmas fern, *Polystichum acrostichoides,* whose lustrous dark green fronds, defying winter's winds and snow, make it a favorite with everybody. Though the spores are actually borne on the undersides of the green pinnae (which are not subdivided), they are located only toward the end, and the fruit dots are so closely massed as to produce an impression of solidity quite different from the rest of the frond.

Lacking this feature, but otherwise like a small edition of the Christmas fern, with its undivided and leathery-textured pinnae, is the polypody, *Polypodium virginianum.* But while the Christmas fern is often found in rocky areas, this species invariably grows *on* the face—bare except for a thin covering of moss or lichens—of a ledge or large boulder; and consequently, during dry periods, the fronds curl up and appear dead. But, resupplied with moisture by even a little rain, they resume their pristine appearance, earning the popular name—shared with a few other species—of "resurrection fern."

A similar preference for naked rock, though willing to avail itself of any convenient crack (as near the base of the High Ledge itself) is rusty woodsia, *Woodsia ilvensis,* small, gray-green, resembling in color the rock on which it grows, and hence easy to overlook, but, because of its rarity, always exciting to discover.

An identical habitat is chosen by the true spleenworts, of which two species, the ebony, *Asplenium platyneuron,* and the maidenhair, *Asplenium trichomanes,* have found a home at High Ledges. Though comparisons are odious, and every species of fern offers a distinctive charm, one would hesitate to challenge the judgment that none is so exquisite as the maidenhair spleenwort. The tiny fronds radiating in graceful arcs from the center in some crack or cranny of a vertical rock face, with their shiny, black, threadlike stems, set on each side with a row of irregularly rounded pinnae sized to scale, create a gemlike quality that is unique. The larger fronds of ebony spleenwort, with smooth-edged oblong pinnae, growing more at random, are rare and beautiful but lack the perfect symmetry of the maidenhair spleenwort.

In the same location as the latter, sometimes side by side, occurs another rare and delicate species called the bladder fern or the fragile fern, depending on which part of the scientific name, *Cystopteris fragilis,* one wishes to stress. As compared with the maidenhair spleenwort, the fronds are larger, more intricate in design, and more fragile in texture, pleasing but not striking. A second member of the genus, the bulblet bladder fern, *Cystopteris bulbifera,* prefers to grow on mossy boulders in or along shaded streams. Two unique traits are that the fronds, larger but no less fragile than those of its relative, taper so gradually toward the end as to produce an almost serpentine effect; and that they bear on the underside tiny bulblike structures, which eventually detach themselves, fall, and become the source of new plants.

Finally, if one were to choose a fern more lovely than the maidenhair spleenwort, it would be the maidenhair fern, *Adiantum pedatum,* itself. There is something almost magical in its pattern of growth, which bears no resemblance to that of any other fern. At the summit of the slender, foot-high stem of shining black, arms reach out in opposite directions, then curve around until they almost meet to form a perfect circle, from the rim of which delicate pinnae branch outward like rays, each divided in turn to create a lacelike pattern marvelous in its symmetry.

Once more, in this excursion through the world of ferns, we encounter the dominant theme of nature's symphony—the almost infinite complexity that is revealed by an unhurried attentiveness to the natural environment. And the pleasures, both of the senses and the intellect, that comes with this enhanced awareness makes us conscious, as we follow a woodland trail, of how bare the earth would be without its clothing of ferns, and how restful and refreshing to the spirit is the "green shade" that they help create.

If we can be thus awakened to the wonders of a world that is not made by humans, we may acquire a measure of humility, and free ourselves from the pride of possession that dictates so many of the values, and causes so much of the discord, that characterize our present society.

C H A P T E R   9

Plants without Leaves

I remember that when the ducklings hatched and were taking stock of their surroundings, in Hans Christian Andersen's fairy tale "The Ugly Duckling," "the mother let them look, for green is good for the eyes." And, though it may be a fancy born of familiarity, from my earliest days with the New England landscape, it seems to me that green is a color singularly conducive to peace of mind and spirit. Moreover, the green foliage of most flowering plants seems always to harmonize with the colors of their blossoms, whether brilliant or subdued.

Yet the infinitely varied order of nature has a place for plants that are wholly devoid of green.

Some of these—a relative few—are flowering plants that once had green leaves, but that the always mysterious process of evolution has now left leafless, with nothing but some reminiscent scales, white or yellow or brown, along the naked stem.

The most familiar of these is Indian pipes, *Monotropa uniflora,* which in midsummer push their way through the woodland carpet of dead leaves, and whose ghostly presence no eye can miss. Much less common, but equally distinctive, is their close relative, pinesaps or false beechdrops, *Monotropa hypopithys,* similar in the shape of the

flowers but differing in color—pale yellow shading into tan—and in the fact that each stem bears a cluster of flowers instead of only one.

All members of this group, lacking chlorophyll, are unable to manufacture their own food and so must draw it from other sources. If the source is decaying organic matter, they are called saprophytes, if from living organisms, parasites. Indian pipes and pinesaps are in the former category, whereas true beechdrops, *Epifagus virginiana*, a nondescript plant with a weak, slender stem and small inconspicuous white flowers, are described in *Gray's Manual* as either "parasitic or saprophytic," always on the roots of beech trees. A close relative, but one dramatically different in outward appearance, is squawroot, *Conopholis americana*, whose short, thick, fleshy stem, bearing many close-packed small yellowish flowers, has an overall shape suggestive of the cone of a white pine. Its preferred host is the root of an oak tree.

Then there are the coral-roots, *Corallorhiza*, already referred to in the essay on orchids, and the parasitic dodder, *Cuscuta gronovii*, a relative of the morning glory, whose threadlike orange stem, though fragile in appearance, winds itself with strangling force around the stems of other plants while it sucks out their vital fluids.

Though nothing in nature can be unnatural, and organic evolution cannot properly be thought of in terms of progress or retrogression but only change, this loss of self-sufficiency, or creativity, somehow runs counter to our human expectations.

The great majority of leafless plants, however, have not undergone such a seeming reversal of direction and have never possessed flowers or leaves, or chlorophyll to produce their own food, but have followed a dif-

Plants without Leaves

ferent path to survival. These are mushrooms, known to me as a child, in their most common form, by the unromantic name of toadstools.

Mushrooms may not be regarded, strictly speaking, as "plants." But, as is becoming evident on the frontiers of science, nature resists the human urge to define and compartmentalize; and mushrooms have enough affinities with green plants to justify, perhaps, the title of this essay.

Mushrooms belong to the vast division of living forms called fungi, which are sometimes referred to as the "third kingdom," on an equal footing with the plant and animal kingdoms: no less diverse in its forms and life processes, and no less essential a part of the planet's biosystem.

Like plants, mushrooms have one part above and one part below the surface of the soil—or whatever substance, or entity, may be the host. The visible part is referred to as the fruiting body, and its essential function, as in plants, is reproduction; while the invisible part—a spreading network of fine threadlike elements called the mycelium, analogous to the roots of a green plant—provides the food on which the life of the organism depends.

Though mushrooms make up a relatively small part of the world of fungi, it is the part, in general, of which we are most aware, both from observation and from literature.

Perhaps it is the absence of chlorophyll, which we automatically think of as a defining element of plant life, that leads us initially to look on mushrooms as an alien presence in the living world. Add to this the seeming mystery of their sudden and unexpected appearance in new locations (since the spores by which they reproduce are, unlike most seeds, too minute to catch the human eye and are easily dispersed by currents of air), the seeming paradox that some species are the gourmet's delight while others are deadly if eaten, the fact that some species possess hallucinatory, or mind-altering, properties— and one can understand the unique fascination that these forms of life have had for human beings, as evidenced by their long and widespread association with fairy tales and folklore.

My own interest in them, however, is not anthropological or gastronomic (at the table I can take them or leave them, but much prefer to leave them) but rather as another instance of the infinite variety of nature, a challenge to our understanding, and often, through their many forms and colors, a pleasure to the eye. That is, I am a "micophile" (mushroom lover) rather than a "micophagist" (mushroom eater).

The most familiar type, the source of the popular mental picture, has a fleshy stem surmounted by a circular disk, or cap, suggestive, if slender and graceful, of a parasol, or, if short and stout, of a stool.

This group includes most of the species that, because they are poisonous, attract the most curiosity. Contrary to popular belief, only a few species are fatal, but this does not diminish the need for caution, since there is no general rule for determining, from its observable traits, whether or to what degree a species is poisonous. Indeed, some members of a genus may be edible and others deadly. This is most notoriously true of the *Amanitas*, which can usually be identified by a sort of collar, or ring, just below the cap, and the fact that the bulbous base of the stem is set in a sort of cup, called the volva—although this is not always obvious.

Two of the most deadly species are the death cap, *Amanita phalloides,* and the destroying angel, *Amanita virosa.* The toxin that they contain is a kind that destroys the body tissues, especially the liver and kidneys, and is particularly insidious because the symptoms do not appear for several hours, sometimes even a day, and then it is too late for countermeasures, even if there were any known antidote.

On the other hand, some members of the genus are edible, of which perhaps the most famous is Caesar's mushroom, *Amanita caesarea,* popular since the time of the ancient Greeks.

Probably the *Amanita* most familiar to Americans is the fly agaric, *Amanita muscaria,* a large mushroom with a bright orange cap several inches across, sprinkled with white warts, the cap contrasting sharply with the pure white stem and gills. Though widely believed to be deadly,

it has caused few confirmed fatalities. The dominant toxin is the type that affects the nerves rather than destroying the tissues, and can also be fatal, as in some species of the genus *Clitocybe* (though this genus, like *Amanita,* has some edible species). In the fly agaric, however, the effects are mainly hallucinogenic, and it has been widely used in religious rituals in which the participants seek a psychic "high." It is said to have been a popular intoxicant among some Siberian tribes until it was replaced by vodka—presumably because the latter was cheaper and quicker.

Most poisonous mushrooms, however, merely affect the digestive system, producing effects like those caused by various types of "food poisoning," which are unpleasant but rarely fatal.

It is hard to make accurate generalizations about the effects of eating poisonous mushrooms because there are so many variables. One is obviously the amount that has been consumed. Another is that some species that are edible when young become toxic at a later stage while others are more toxic when young. Some species are poisonous when eaten raw but become edible after cooking while others are unaffected. And the same species may produce unpleasant effects in one person but not in another.

I am amused to read notations concerning some species such as "edibility unknown," or "suspected of being poisonous," or "it is advisable to leave these small fungi alone."

As I have said, however, it is the visual characteristics of mushrooms, their form and color, that chiefly arouse my interest. The range of colors, indeed, rivals that of flowers: some are pure white; some buff or pale brown; some yellow, varying in shade from bright gold to dull or dirty; some scarlet at their first appearance, fading as they grow to a delicate pink; some ranging from pale lilac to deep purple; some brilliant orange; some golden brown. Once, even, I found a clump that was sky blue. And, despite their lack of chlorophyll, some manage to achieve a tinge of green. Finally, while composing this essay, I noticed for the first time a mushroom (short, thick-stemmed, and clustered) that was solid black.

Particularly notable for brightly colored species is the genus *Russula*. But in general there seems to be little connection between color and genus, or between color and edibility.

Equally diverse, and of course essential to identification, are the forms of the different genera and species. Even those belonging to the familiar parasol type have caps that show enormous variation. Some are almost perfectly flat; some are convex in varying degrees; others— or the same species at a later stage—are more or less concave. Some may have a sort of nipple at the center; others may have a hollow. Some are smooth on the upper surface; others may have a few or many warts; a few have a netted appearance.

Most of the members of this group have gills on the underside of the cap, conveying an impression of fragility. Usually they are white, as is the stem, and they often offer a dramatic contrast to the brightly colored cap. But, as always, there are exceptions to the general rule, and in some species the cap and the stem are of one solid color.

In some other species, notably of the common genus *Boletus,* the underside of the cap is smooth and seemingly solid, but a close inspection reveals that the surface is broken by a multitude of tiny pores. Some members of this genus grow to a relatively enormous size. I have a slide in which the ends of a foot rule, placed in front of the cap, coincide almost exactly with its outer edges.

In either case, gills or pores, it is these structures that produce the spores by which the organisms reproduce.

Many genera, however, abandon completely the parasol or toadstool pattern. One is *Morchella,* to which belongs the famous morel— the source of many tales of intense rivalry among seekers for the ambrosial prize. I myself have never found it at High Ledges—or, in fact, anywhere else—but pictures of it suggest, to me, the image of a cone-shaped sponge. Another group has a shape indicated by the genus name, *Phallus*. Very different are the delicate club mushrooms, typical genus *Clavaria,* whose slender stalk, usually about two inches high in the specimens that I have observed, in color white or yellow, may become larger toward the top, so as to suggest, indeed, a lilliputian club. On the same scale are the coral mushrooms, for example, genus *Clavulina* or *Ramaria,* composed of clusters of close-packed, tiny, vertical stems—white, bright yellow, or, as I have occasionally observed, deep purple.

Differing greatly in size and shape are the sturdy chanterelles, genus *Cantharellus,* common and prized for their agreeable taste and characterized by a fruiting body that resembles an inverted cone, flared at the top like a horn. Following an opposite pattern are the cup mushrooms (usually *Peziza*), whose stemless fruiting bodies, almost paper thin, are curled inward at the top to form a wide-based, shallow cup.

It may come as a surprise that puffballs (comprising a variety of genera), noticed most often at their mature stage when the tough, brown skin of the small sphere bursts open to release a cloud of dark spores, are also mushrooms; and at an earlier stage of growth, the interior consists of firm, white, often edible flesh.

Finally (leaving aside an almost endless number of other groups and subgroups), there are the shelf fungi, growing out from the trunks of dead or diseased trees, which have many of the properties of mushrooms. They vary as greatly in size and color, and to a lesser extent in form, while retaining the general shape that the name implies. And they reproduce in the same fashion as the parasol-type mushrooms,

shedding their spores from the underside of the "shelf." (On a fallen tree, if they are at right angles to the trunk, one knows that they were formed before it fell; if they are parallel to the line of the trunk, it is evident that their growth followed its fall.) And, although some of the larger species are almost as hard as their host, others, at a certain stage, are edible.

This chapter was read in its original form by Dr. Gail Schumann, who made several helpful suggestions.

Epilogue

This book has offered only a glimpse of one small area of the living world that High Ledges—a Sanctuary in many senses of the word—offers to those who wish to escape from the pressures of the outer world. But the word "escape" is misleading. Rather, one is invited to enter another world, where the values are other than material and the impulses other than acquisitive.

One of them is curiosity about the natural world—of which, though we often forget it, we and all our works are inescapably a part. Indeed, one of the defining traits of the human species is the capacity to consciously observe the world around us, along with the urge to establish some order, some system of relationships, among the infinite number of distinct perceptions that crowd our existence. It is in this urge that we find the origin of modern science, which has been defined as "organized knowledge."

We tend to assume that the main motive behind this impulse is a practical one, the desire to master and manage the natural world so as to enhance our comfort and security. But some people like to think that there is another motive even more basic: the instinctive attraction—one might even call it "love"—of knowledge for its own sake. Aristotle's wisdom was never more evident than in his dictum, "All men [that is, all human beings] desire to know." And though many forces in modern society tend to obscure and minimize this desire, the recognition of it can, beyond question, contribute to the enrichment of our existence.

A second ultimate value, not susceptible to analysis and not to be thought of in terms of anything other than itself, is beauty. As Emerson says in his simple and exquisite poem "The Rhodora," ". . . beauty is its own excuse for being."

It is these values that High Ledges Wildlife Sanctuary offers in full measure to those who seek them.

Index